PASS YOUR MOTORCYCLE L TEST

John Robinson

RIGHT WAY

CONTENTS

Preface

If you are looking for a short cut to passing your riding test then I'm afraid you have come to the wrong place.

This book sets out the things you need to know and the skills you need to develop, in order to ride a bike a bit more than just competently. If you can ride well, you will pass the test. But you have to do it yourself, no-one can do it for you.

You need the information, which you can find here and in the Highway Code; you need to practise a lot – this can't be over-emphasised; and you need expert tuition because you won't always realise when you are doing something wrong (or omitting to do something right).

Most people fail driving tests because they are not ready; either they haven't practised machine control enough or they have been misinformed and they make mistakes – not looking behind at the right moment is a classic.

You have to be so familiar with your machine that operating it is second nature. You have to know how to operate it for the maximum safety of yourself and those around you. Finally you have to demonstrate this knowledge in front of an examiner. That's how to pass the test, and it isn't difficult.

The rest is about enjoying your new freedom and living long enough to enjoy it.

A separate, theory part of the L test is anticipated for the second half of the 90s. Like Compulsory Basic Training, you will probably have to pass this before you can take any bike out on the road.

Readers of this book will be well equipped to answer the set questions. They will probe your understanding of the theory and practicalities of riding (as set out in this book) and will assess your reactions to given situations – especially those which are less likely to come up during your on-road test.

What you absorb from these pages will help you answer these questions correctly. Further questions may test your knowledge of the Highway Code and traffic law, which is covered in the special section at the back of the Highway Code.

1
Riding Tests

When driving licences were first thought of, it was enough merely to buy one. Later, a rudimentary test was developed which, for motorcyclists, consisted of a crude eye test, observed riding in traffic, an emergency stop, a slow riding test and a few questions based on the *Highway Code*. Anyone from the age of 16 could ride any size of bike. If you passed a car driving test, it automatically qualified you to ride a moped. Unlike learner car drivers, bike riders did not have to be supervised by a qualified passenger but they could only carry a passenger who held a full bike licence.

The same basic test remained until the 'pursuit' test was introduced in 1991, although it was subject to more and more restrictions.

First, learners were restricted to 250cc solo machines (but any size was permitted if a sidecar was attached). The minimum age limit was raised to 17 (but 16 for a moped; after 1 August 1977 the definition of "moped" changed from up-to-50cc with pedals into up-to-50cc with a design top speed of 30mph ±5mph).

The next restriction was to 125cc (except with sidecars) with a power limit of 9kW (which is 12.07 horsepower) and a maximum power-to-weight ratio of 100kW/tonne. If the machine was registered before 31 December 1982 then it need only be of 125cc or less. In practice this restriction gives a top speed of 65 to 70mph, with acceleration roughly the same as most family saloon cars. From 1983 on, 125cc machines are supposed to have a plate fixed to the frame, denoting their make, model, size, weight and power output.

The test itself was revised into a two-part affair, Part 1 being a riding control test on an off-road area, while Part 2 was much the same as before, with an observer watching from the kerbside and afterwards, a few *Highway Code* questions. Logically, Part 1 had to be passed before Part 2 and if this wasn't passed within two years, the licence was suspended for one year.

This was all revised again in 1991. The requirements at the time

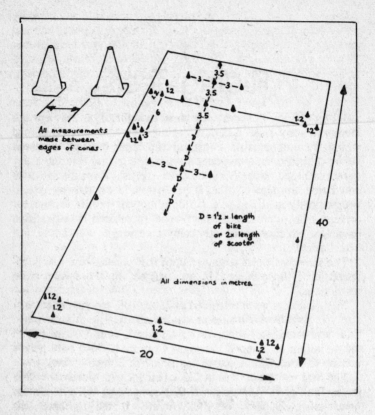

Fig. 1. This is the layout of the area for the old Part 1 test, which is no longer a requirement for learner riders, but sections of it make useful practice in machine control. The overall dimensions may be altered to fit whatever area is available but note the distances between cones (or any suitable markers) for the brake test and the slalom tests.

of publication (early 1992) are:

Age 16: moped only (up to 50cc, limited to 30mph), even if test is passed.

Age 17-on: provisional licence (learner) restricted 125cc solo (12bhp) or smaller, but any capacity if a sidecar is attached. A solo rider may not carry a passenger, but a sidecar driver may carry a passenger in the sidecar, assuming that it is constructed to take a passenger.

On passing the test on a motorcycle you may ride any capacity motorcycle, solo or sidecar or a moped, without L-plates and you may carry passengers. They must sit astride and have proper footrests. On passing the test on a moped, you are only entitled to ride a moped (without L-plates and with a passenger as above).

Provisional licence-holders must display regulation-sized L-plates at the front and rear of their machines. (Note that these should be fitted flat and in a near-vertical position, which is not always easy to do on a motorcycle; your dealer may be able to help by making up a suitable bracket or supplying rigid plates which can be bolted onto a convenient mounting point.)

Licences: no-one with a provisional bike or moped licence may take to the road until they have completed the Compulsory Basic Training course (CBT) and have the certificate which says so. (How to obtain this certificate will be explained shortly.) This applies to mopeds, solos and bikes with sidecars, but if you have passed CBT in one category it is not necessary to repeat it, for example, if you move from a moped to a 125cc solo. The CBT certificate is valid for three years. The provisional licence may be exchanged for a full licence after passing the Accompanied (or 'pursuit') Test, observed by a Department of Transport examiner.

Tests (for more detailed requirements, see below): The 'pursuit' test is on public roads; the examiner follows behind on a motorcycle (or in a car in certain circumstances) and gives instructions to the testee through a (sterilized) radio headset which is provided. To apply for this test, and see an up-to-date list of its requirements, use forms DL26 and D100, from any post office. The CBT certificate must be included in the test application. To apply for a driving licence in the first place, use form D1. You can get more information from DVLA Driver Enquiry Unit at Swansea SA6 7JL, telephone 0792 772151.

If you do not pass a test within two years, then your provisional motorcycle licence will be suspended for 12 months.

Exceptions:

1. Riders in remote islands may not have to take CBT (Compulsory Basic Training), but may only ride in their own locality without it.

2. Passing a car driving test also gives a full moped licence.

3. A full car licence issued before 1 December 1990 also acts as a motorcycle provisional licence and (subject to the 125cc/12bhp solo limit and use of L-plates) the holder can ride a motorcycle without passing the CBT and without the 12-month licence suspension every two years. However, before taking the motorcycle test, it will be necessary to obtain a CBT certificate.

4. Full car licences issued after 1 December 1990 do not permit the use of a motorcycle without the CBT certificate.

5. Holders of full licences for groups other than motorcycles do not suffer the 12-month suspension if the test is not passed in a two-year period. So if your provisional bike licence is suspended, it is worth taking a provisional licence for another group (mopeds is an obvious choice) and passing your test for this group at which point you will be allowed to renew your motorcycle provisional licence.

6. The 12-month suspension can be avoided, or at least postponed, if you surrender your provisional licence to the DVLA at Swansea. In the event of illness, work abroad or some other good reason to prevent you riding in this country, the licence can be surrendered and re-started when you are able to ride, so if it was surrendered for three months, there would be three months added to the two-year period.

Obviously things can change and the trend is towards more restrictions, so it is worth checking the current requirements either from the DVLA Swansea or from test application forms at main post offices.

Likely developments are to "harmonize" regulations between European countries, and progressive licensing for more powerful machines. One example which has been discussed is that riders who have passed the test should be restricted for two years to machines which produce no more than 33bhp and have a maximum power to weight ratio of 160kW/tonne. In Japan, riders already have to take a separate test to move up to 400cc and then 750cc machines.

Training centres can be found via local dealers, motorcycle clubs, advertisements in the motorcycle press, council road safety offices, via the organisations listed in the Appendix (page 121) or in the Yellow Pages telephone directory.

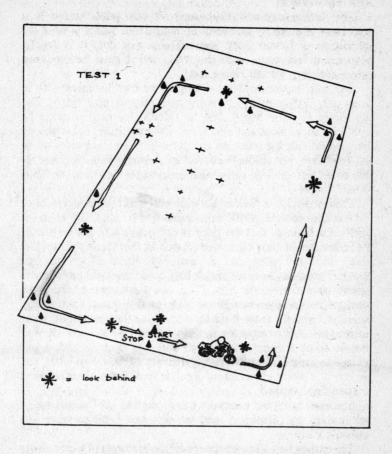

TEST 1

STOP

START

❋ = look behind

Fig. 2. The simplest exercise (formerly Test 1) is to pull away and follow a marked course (a rectangular one in this case), manoeuvring between cones, which have gaps of 1.2 metres, and stopping the bike at a specified point. The rider has reached a reasonable level of expertise when he can pull away smoothly, look behind and indicate before changing direction, stopping or starting. He should accelerate, brake and change gear smoothly, and find neutral just as the machine comes to a standstill. The machine should be controlled with both brakes, using 1st gear for the tight corners and changing into 2nd and possibly 3rd along the straights. It should not be necessary to put a foot down until the machine stops.

Test requirements

CBT: before any new rider sets out onto public roads it is necessary to reach a basic level of competence which is what the certificate of Compulsory Basic Training is for. It is legally required before going onto the road, and it must be produced when applying for the riding test.

Any full licence-holder working at an establishment with at least one DoT-qualified instructor can instruct new riders. The instructor must be happy that the rider is (a) familiar with the controls, adjustment and operation of the machine, (b) is able to handle and ride the machine competently (riding exercises on an off-road area, not unlike the exercises shown in Figs. 1-5) and (c) has been instructed in, and ridden under supervision in, traffic on public roads.

The instruction is divided between practical tuition and lectures on machine control, traffic regulations and so on. Only when the instructor believes that the rider is competent will the certificate be issued, so the time taken will depend on the rider's ability. Note that, until the rider has a certificate, it is illegal to ride unsupervised on the road, which may cause practical problems in getting to and from the site. There are ways around this: some dealers have a large enough car park or free space for training; some will deliver to the training area a bike they have sold; some instructors will arrange for the supervised ride to finish at your home; some training centres will hire out bikes so riders can complete their CBT before taking delivery of their own bikes, and so on. It is worth checking on possible local arrangements before committing yourself.

You must take your insurance certificate and MoT certificate (if applicable) and display a road tax disc and L-plates when you attend CBT.

The earlier Part 1 test contained all the elements of Compulsory Basic Training. For this reason, in this chapter, you will find a series of five drawings (Figs. 1-5) with captions which explain what used to be done. If you are able to follow these manoeuvres on private ground or at the place where you do your CBT, at the end of it you will know that you have reached the necessary standard.

Accompanied Test ('pursuit' test)

This follows the same format as the original − later the Part 2 − test except that the examiner now follows on another bike and is able to observe you all the time. A one-way radio link allows

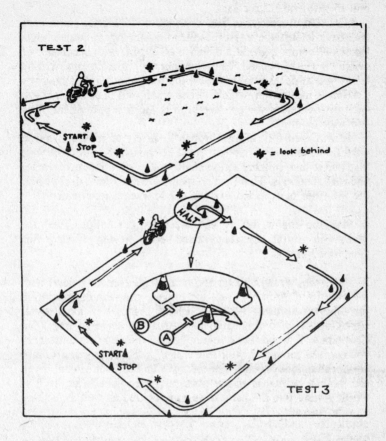

Fig. 3. The old Tests 2 and 3 included reversing the course direction (being able to turn the bike around in a small area) and stopping at one of the turns. The bike must not overshoot the "Halt" line and the rider must be able to pull away smoothly, while turning. Planning ahead and good road positioning make this easier; for example, stopping at point A would make for a tighter turn than point B. Stop with your right foot down, stretched slightly forward so that, as the bike begins to move, it can pivot around it, moving away with just one push from your foot – not in a series of hops. Don't paddle along. This will make you wobble. Select 1st gear and keep one foot on the footrest, giving a gentle push with the other as the bike gains momentum and balance. Which foot depends on the direction of turn or whether you need to use the back brake (on a slope).

him to give you instructions.

The usual procedure is first to have the radio fitted and tested, and to complete the eye test (be able to read standard number plate figures (79.4mm high) at a distance of 20.5m, with spectacles or contact lenses if needed. The examiner will also explain what he wants you to do: typically, follow the road ahead unless he gives a different instruction, which will be given well in advance. If you become separated, you are to pull in at the first convenient place and wait for him.

He will then follow you through a variety of road and traffic conditions, where you are expected to show full control of your bike and to take suitable action to allow for other traffic, obstacles and road junctions. There are no specific criteria for a pass or fail, but the rider is expected to meet the following requirements:

1. Start the engine, taking any necessary precautions (fuel on, gearbox in neutral, side-stand raised before moving off, etc.). See Chapters 3 and 4.

2. Pull away, straight ahead and at an angle (see 11. below) with full control of throttle, clutch and brakes, and with consideration for other road users — look behind before any manoeuvre, signalling in good time and not getting in anyone's way. (See Chapters 4, 7, 8 and 10.) Looking behind: in many circumstances you can see enough in your mirrors; if you have any doubt, turn your head to look around. The only way an observer can tell if you are looking behind is if you physically turn your head, so it is worth getting into the habit of turning behind as well as looking in your mirrors.

3. Overtake, meet and cross the path of other traffic and take an appropriate course (which includes all-round vision and signalling your intentions). See Chapters 7, 8 and 10.

4. Turn right- and left-hand corners (junctions) correctly: correct approach, road positioning and signals. See Chapter 7.

5. Stop the bike in an emergency. The examiner will not follow, but will stand at the roadside, making sure the traffic conditions are safe, then he will step out and hold one hand up, at which point you should stop as quickly as possible yet under full control. He is looking for quick reactions, proper use of both brakes, the ability to stop without skidding or to correct and release a minor

skid quickly. During other parts of the test you will also be asked to stop, and should be able to stop the bike normally, pulling up in a suitable part of the road. See Chapter 5.

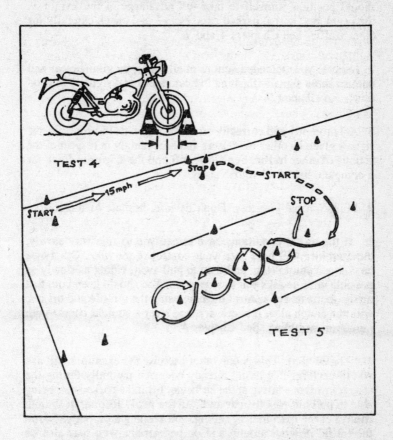

Fig. 4. The former test 4 was a braking control test, not an emergency stop. From about 15mph you should be able to brake gently and stop the bike so that the front wheel is exactly inside the box. It is instructive to vary the speed and brake pressure and to experiment using the front brake only, rear brake only and both brakes together. Change down into 1st gear while braking and stop, either with the clutch lifted, still in gear, or, as you gain skill, shift into neutral as the wheels stop rolling. The old test 5 was a slalom; you can take wide lines or tight lines but you mustn't go beyond the outer markers or touch a marker. Experiment by varying the distance between markers; plan ahead by taking a wide loop at each end to put you easily on your chosen line.

6. Turn the machine round to face the opposite direction (U-turn). Again, the examiner will watch from the roadside. The road will normally be wide enough for a complete U-turn but you should position yourself to take full advantage of the terrain — road cambers, kerbs, parked cars, etc. — and check carefully for other traffic. See Chapters 4 and 7.

7. Indicate your intended actions at all times, by giving clear and unmistakable signals (flashing indicators or hand signals) in good time. See Chapter 7.

8. Act promptly and correctly on traffic signs, traffic controls, the signals given by other road users and accordingly in respect of the actions of other traffic. See Chapter 8 and the *Highway Code* for a complete list of all traffic signs.

9. Make normal progress. Don't dawdle, hesitate or dither.

10. If the traffic conditions have forced you to ride very slowly, the examiner will have seen your control of the bike. Otherwise he will ask you to stop, and then to pull away, riding as slowly as possible until he asks you to stop again. You should keep both feet on the footrests and control the bike using the throttle and brakes, with the clutch also, if necessary, and steer a straight course with minimum wobbling. See Chapter 4.

11. Angled start. This is one other exercise the examiner will ask you to perform if it hasn't already occurred naturally during the test. It involves starting at the kerbside, behind a parked car, being able to pull out past the car and join the road, keeping in smooth control of the machine, signalling, and keeping a proper check on the traffic flow all around and on pedestrians who may also be waiting for a break in the traffic in order to cross the road — possibly from behind the parked car. See Chapter 4.

12. After returning to the test centre and removing the radio, you will be asked questions based on the *Highway Code*, which may include details of other types of traffic, e.g. what do white lights showing on the rear of a car signify (reversing lights) and on stopping distances, as well as road signs, mandatory speed limits and so on. See the *Highway Code*.

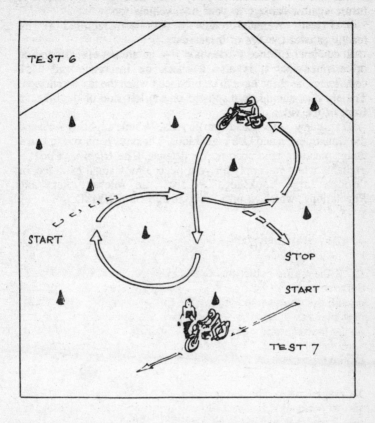

Fig. 5. A figure-8 course can be made harder, to match your level of skill. Former test 6 was a matter of circulating the figure-8 until asked to stop. Experiment with different lines and by accelerating/braking gently as well as manoeuvring at a steady speed. The earlier test 7 is a slow riding test in which you keep pace with someone walking, and you may need to ease the clutch in and out to prevent the engine jerking or stalling. This can be applied to both the slalom and the figure-8 courses — try following them as slowly as possible, keeping smooth control of the bike without putting a foot down.

Other legal requirements (see Chapter 2 for more detailed information):

Helmet — required for all riders and passengers, except passengers in sidecars.

Insurance — against third party risks, although it is possible to insure against damage to your own vehicle too.

MoT test — annual roadworthiness test, required for all machines over the age of three years.

Road Fund Licence ("road tax") — an annual tax, depending on engine size. It is also a check on insurance and MoT certificates, as these have to be produced when the tax is renewed. The tax disc should be displayed on the left side of the bike, in front of the rider.

Traffic law — the Road Traffic Acts, Vehicle Lighting Acts and the Construction and Use regulations. The onus is on you to know them; pleading ignorance isn't a defence. The *Highway Code* — available when you apply for your licence for a small extra fee, or through large bookshops — lists the relevant Acts and Regulations, which in turn are available from HMSO.

2
Getting Started

Before getting involved with the niceties of machine control or the subtleties of riding examinations, before you even take to the road, there is whole list of things you will need. Some are more obvious than others, many are not quite as straightforward as they seem and all of them will cost money. Eventually they will have to be budgeted for and it is worth having a look at all the implications right at the start so that if you have to start cutting corners you can do it in a way that will not cause too much embarrassment later on.

The main items are:

1. Bike (you will need the owner's handbook too).
2. Insurance.
3. An MoT roadworthiness test if the bike is three or more years old.
4. Road fund licence.
5. Helmet plus visor or goggles.
6. Other protective clothing.
7. L-plates, a provisional licence and a working knowledge of traffic laws.
8. Somewhere to ride.

1. BIKE

Seems obvious enough yet there are several potential pitfalls to watch out for. There are restrictions as to what type of bike you may learn on, explained on pages 6 and 18. You will need a receipt when you buy it, as proof of ownership. Your legal rights can be affected quite seriously here. A used machine may be sold "as seen" and the seller may put words to this effect on the receipt. This means that you accept it as you see it, including any faults. Normally it would be hard to blame any defects on a private seller but a dealer or anyone who could be considered an expert could justifiably be asked to make good any faults — unless they had been pointed out before the sale was agreed. In this case the receipt would also need to say that the machine was not roadworthy or not in running order.

The registration document (or "log" book) is simply that, no more and no less; it describes and identifies the bike along with the "keeper" of the machine. It does not prove ownership, but be very careful if there is not a registration document or if there is any sort of problem. Check that the details tally with the bike and check that the mileage recorded on any MoT certificates looks reasonable. Possible problems here include machines still subject to HP (which belong to the finance company in law), stolen machines and machines which have been written off in a crash and subsequently rebuilt.

On receiving the bike you should complete the "change of ownership" section on the registration document and send it off − full instructions are printed on it.

If the money for the machine is coming from a finance deal, hire purchase or a loan, be certain of the conditions and of your ability to honour the actual repayments. Any doubts should be referred to a professional adviser, such as your bank manager.

Make sure you have a clear understanding of any warranty or servicing arrangements with the machine. If the machine is still under the manufacturer's warranty, this will usually be transferred to a new owner. Dealers will often offer their own guarantee with a low-mileage bike; it is also possible to buy extended warranty − a sort of insurance against specified mechanical failures. The dealer will also offer service facilities (the first service is usually free on new machines, apart from oil or other materials needed).

Despite the claims made by manufacturers and importers, it can be very difficult to get spare parts on quite a few models, depending on whereabouts you live. It is worth making a few discreet enquiries − from other riders and local clubs − to check on your local spares' availability.

Riders who are 16 years old are restricted to mopeds, which now means any two-wheeler with an engine of less than 50cc, a maximum design speed of 30mph (±5 mph) and which carries a homologation plate on the frame. Machines registered before 1 August 1977 are mopeds if they have an engine of less than 50cc and have pedals which can propel them.

Learner riders of 17 and over are restricted to machines of up to 125cc: if the bike was registered after 31 December 1982 then it must also be restricted to 9kW (12bhp) under specified conditions and must not exceed 100kW/tonne. It must also carry a plate on its frame. For bikes registered before this date, the 125cc limit is the only restriction.

There is only one exception. Learners who are 17 or more can ride a motorcycle and sidecar of any capacity provided they hold a CBT (Compulsory Basic Training) certificate.

However, despite the apparent similarities, a combination motorcycle/sidecar is generally a totally different vehicle to drive and is not covered by this book. Having said that, there are a very few sidecars which are mounted on a parallelogram linkage so that they can lean with the motorcycle. The only one in production in the U.K. is sold under the name Sidewinder. It is not constructed to carry a passenger and, apart from the increased width of the vehicle, it lets the machine behave just like a solo. Learners can quite legally fit one of these to any size of machine.

Finally, trailers. From 1983, solo motorcycles were allowed to tow trailers which conformed to certain regulations, namely that their weight did not exceed 150kg or two-thirds of the motorcycle's weight, that their width did not exceed 1 metre and that the length from the bike's back axle to the rear of the trailer did not exceed 2.5 metres; there is also a 50mph restriction and the trailer must not be towed by a machine of 125cc or less — effectively ruling out learner riders. In fact new learners are prohibited from towing a trailer with any category of vehicle.

Within these restrictions, there is a further choice, dictated largely by finance — new, nearly new or getting on in years. A new or new-ish bike offers the least complication but it is still worth a check on parts and availability, re-selling prices and insurance. A used bike should be inspected by someone who can vouch for its safety and mechanical soundness, especially if no warranty is being offered with it. Notice that your best buy may depend more upon the existence of a reliable local dealer, than on any supposed merits of competing designs of bike. The final option of an old or well-worn machine is fine provided that you have the facilities to keep it roadworthy.

If you have access to private land, an old banger is probably the best way to learn although insurance-wise it would be at your own risk. Even if it is only ridden on private land, however, you still need a licence and all the other legal requirements just to stand or push it on a public highway (the paths and verges as well as the road). Ironically, if the bike is put on a small trolley, it can be pushed legally along the road without insurance etc.

To avoid the nuisance of having to buy a learner-restricted bike which will then be sold as soon as the test is passed, it is possible to hire machines from some test centres, for lessons and the test itself. Backed up by practice on an old banger on private land to develop your co-ordination and riding control, this could be the cheapest and most convenient way to take the test.

Don't forget you will need the owner's handbook for the bike — for details such as tyre pressures and other adjustments you may need to make. As well as showing the layout and operation of the controls, this will also show items such as the electrical wiring, position and type of fuse, type of oils and methods of checking the correct levels. These things vary from make to make and it is important to learn as much as you possibly can about the machine before trying to use it.

2. INSURANCE

This can often be a major expense, especially for a youngster running a motorcycle. A certain level of cover is legally required (called "Act only" — referring to the Road Traffic Act) which insures you against damage done to other people. As you could still be sued for damage done to their property, more cover is desirable (you might hit a Rolls-Royce).

This comes in the form of Third Party insurance — covering any damage caused by you to someone else's person or property. (You and the insurance company make the first and second parties, anyone else becomes a third party.)

For slightly more cost this cover can be extended to "Third Party, Fire and Theft". This includes damage done by fire or if the bike is stolen. Check on the exact terms, though — does the policy mean damage done while being stolen, even if you get the bike back afterwards? Does it include things stolen from the bike? Are accessories and luggage included?

The most expensive cover is "Fully Comprehensive". This gives the same cover against damage done to other people, plus damage inflicted on your own machine if you fall off, or if it is knocked over while parked, etc. Once again it is important to check on the exact terms. Many policies have an "excess" — that is you pay the first £x of any claim, where x is usually £25, £50 or £100 (simply to discourage small claims) or more (if you have a bad record).

There will be a list of exceptions, such as civil disturbances and acts of God. You may be allowed to ride other bikes — but often the amount of cover is reduced — and similarly other people may be allowed to ride your bike but not always.

The insurance can be invalidated by certain things, such as a false statement or omission on the proposal form, or not maintaining the machine properly (badly worn tyres are a favourite).

There is a practice among some insurers of limiting the policy to the value of the bike. If the bike is a total loss ("written off" or stolen) and they pay its value (which they will argue is less than what you paid for it), then the policy terminates. You could have a bike stolen the day after you bought it, claim (most of) your money back from the insurer, buy a replacement bike and you might think the remaining 364 days' insurance cover would transfer automatically... you might be wrong. Find out first.

Injuries to yourself may not be covered — you can take out fairly cheap personal accident insurance, but make sure it does not exclude motorcycling!

It is in your best interests to shop around, not only to get the best price but to get the cover you need and to make sure you understand exactly what you have got. A good broker will be able to explain the details and several insurance companies have recently taken to writing their policies in plain English.

3. MoT TEST

Although the name Ministry of Transport exists no more, the triple triangle logo displayed by testing stations is still the sign of an MoT test. When your motorcycle becomes three years old, it must pass this basic roadworthiness check, each year.

Many machines fail because their owners have not bothered to replace a faulty part such as a light bulb, or adjust a brake or something equally simple.

If the machine does not have a current MoT certificate, you may still ride it to your local MoT test station, provided you have an appointment for a test. As you need the MoT certificate to renew the road fund licence, this means that you can ride the machine un-taxed to and from the test centre, but only for the purposes of getting it tested.

To avoid the difficulties of tax, test and insurance all expiring at the same time, you are allowed to have a machine re-rested after 11 months although the certificate will still be dated as if it had been tested on the original expiry date.

Having said that, it is necessary to add that an MoT certificate is not evidence of roadworthiness! So don't rely on a test certificate when you are buying a bike.

4. ROAD FUND LICENCE

"Road tax" — is simply a means of collecting tax and has little nowadays to do with roads or transport. The coloured disc which shows the expiry date must be clearly displayed on the nearside (left side) of the machine, in front of the rider.

To renew it you need to fill in an appropriate form (from a post office or vehicle licensing centre; a reminder, including this form is normally sent from the DVLA Swansea). This, accompanied by evidence of insurance (the certificate, not the policy), an MoT certificate (if necessary) and the money (depending on size of bike) should be taken or sent to a vehicle licensing centre.

These are listed on the renewal forms or, if the tax is being renewed without a break, it can be done at a main post office.

5. HELMET

Motorcycle riders and passengers are legally required to wear a helmet in the U.K.; the helmet should conform to BS6658-85 (or subsequent) British Standard, or be of a similar standard. A retailer may only sell helmets which conform to the standard, although there are shops which legitimately sell other helmets, e.g. for competition use, for car racing, etc. The user has more freedom, as long as the helmet is of a similar standard; that is, well constructed, in good condition, properly fitted and so on. There are exemptions for sidecar passengers and individual exemptions on medical or religious grounds.

Legalities aside, you should get the best helmet you can afford, concentrating on comfort and fit. They give good weather protection as well as defending your head in a crash. Some helmets are made from glass fibre, others from ABS and some from polycarbonate. Plastic materials should not be painted or have stickers put on them, as the helmet can be seriously weakened by the adhesive. Helmets in any event should be replaced every one or two years or whenever they have been damaged.

To go with the helmet, some form of eye protection is essential. Good quality goggles or a plastic visor which clips to the helmet should be used. Don't use one which is scratched, even lightly — the distortion caused by approaching headlamps after dark can seriously reduce vision. Tinted lenses reduce your ability to pick out changes in road surfaces, especially wet areas which could be slippery. There is a British Standard for visors (BS4110XA/YA/ZA) and you should note that tinted visors may only be used in daylight (ironically, it legally is all right to remove them and use nothing!).

Goggles and visors tend to mist over, especially on wet days. This can be prevented to a degree by rubbing liquid soap or antimist compound (from accessory shops) onto the inside surface of the lens.

6. CLOTHING

In our U.K. climate motorcycle clothing has to give good weather protection as well as being strong enough to minimise cuts and grazes if you happen to fall off. It can amount to a major expense so it is worth taking a long look at the available alternatives.

Basically you'll need boots, a riding suit and/or a waterproof oversuit and gloves.

Leather boots are the most comfortable and give some support around the ankles as a safety measure. They range from heavy motorcross boots through stiff-topped touring boots to soft-topped racing boots.

One disadvantage with leather is that it is not waterproof. Rubber boots are both cheap and water-resistant, but not so smart or comfortable. One possible answer is lightweight rubber overboots, which stretch over normal boots or shoes.

A leather riding suit gives good crash protection but is not so good against cold and wet. Two-piece cotton or nylon suits are available with quilted linings (using glass fibre and metal foil) which are very warm. There are also lined and unlined one-piece suits. Waterproofing qualities vary: typically a suit will start to leak after a period which could be as short as a month or as long as a year. Someone who plans a lot of long journeys would find a good quality suit well worth the extra cost. Many oversuits now have bright colours and retro-reflective strips which add a measure of safety.

Finally with gloves make sure that they are comfortable and do not bunch up in the palm when you grip the handlebars. Lined or unlined, gloves made specially for motorcycling usually have the seams on the outside, so that they do not chafe your skin. For weather protection make sure the gloves are long enough to fit under the sleeves of your oversuit. Mittens are undoubtedly warmer in winter but they reduce the amount of control. Alternatives for cold-hand sufferers are electrically heated inner gloves, electrically heated handlebar grips and large muffs which fit over the handlebars.

7. LICENCE

The licensing laws for motorcycle riders have been much amended and made rather confusing. The details as at the close of 1991 have been set out in Chapter 1, and in this chapter in section 1. Always double-check current regulations on your licence application form (from post offices) and, if need be, with your local Road Safety Officer, or with a training course instructor.

Take care to fill in any sections relating to the type of vehicle as there is a difference between licences for bikes and other vehicles. This is because a motorcycle learner who does not pass his pursuit test within two years of taking out the provisional licence will usually have the licence withdrawn for one year.

As for other legal requirements, the onus is on you, as soon as you become a Learner rider, to know and abide by relevant laws. The *Highway Code* is a good starting point. It isn't law in itself, but provides a reference to the various laws as well as explaining the code of practice and road signs. In the event of any legal action it is advisable to seek expert advice from one of the motoring organisations, a Citizens' Advice Bureau or a solicitor.

8. SOMEWHERE TO RIDE

Apart from those holding a full car licence since before December 1990, you have to begin at a training centre off the public road to get your certificate of Compulsory Basic Training. Even those with such a licence have to have a CBT certificate before they can take the motorcycle L-test so really that is the place for everyone to start (see page 10). Expert tuition at such a riding school, backed up by frequent practice, is the quickest way to learn. You should aim to put in one or preferably two half-hour sessions every day. This will develop the co-ordination and the confidence you need to handle the machine safely.

Once your CBT certificate has been obtained, you may legally ride on public roads, except that no learners (and no mopeds) are allowed on motorways. Aim to extend your road experience gradually, no more than half-an-hour to an hour's ride at a time, keeping to lightly-trafficked areas to begin with. Read up your *Highway Code* and all of this book thoroughly before you set out on your own.

3

Pre-ride Checks, Controls, Gear Ratios

Pretty well all motorcycles made since the 1960s have a uniform control layout and even machines made long before do not vary that much.

Figs. 6 and 7 show the positions of typical controls on a modern machine but you should also use the bike's handbook or, better still, have the dealer check you out on your particular machine.

THROTTLE CONTROL

Starting at the handlebar, on the right there is the throttle twistgrip. This handgrip rotates and turning it back towards the rider (counter clockwise as you look at the off-side — or right-hand side as you sit on it — of the bike) opens an air valve to the engine's intake. Allowing the engine more air lets it produce more power; it speeds up and is able to propel the machine faster.

The twistgrip and its cable should be free to move smoothly, and to close without any restriction. Usually the control will open against spring pressure, so when you let go, it will automatically snap closed. Some machines have a friction screw which can be tightened up to hold the throttle in a fixed position — this has some value on long motorway journeys for instance but for learning it is better not to use it.

Make sure that the cable is adjusted properly, so that there is not too much slack in the cable and that the cable is routed so that it cannot be stretched when the handlebars are turned. As easy learning, and, later on, proficient riding, skills all depend upon precise throttle control and rapid response, don't let a sloppy adjuster or a stiff cable make life any harder than it need be.

STARTER SWITCH AND "EMERGENCY" STOP

On the throttle drum there will be a switch — the engine "kill" switch. This is usually marked "RUN — STOP". It shorts out the ignition and is intended to be used to stop the engine in an emergency.

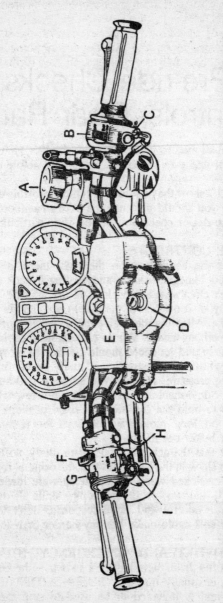

Fig. 6. Typical handlebar control layout. *On the right side:* throttle twistgrip and front brake lever, master cylinder reservoir (A), ignition kill switch (B), starter button (C). *In the centre:* choke control (D), ignition switch/steering lock (E), speedometer with resettable trip, rev. counter, warning lights between dials (indicators, neutral, oil pressure, generator, headlamp main beam). *On the left:* lighting switch (F), dip switch (G), indicator switch (H), horn button (I), headlamp flasher (if fitted), clutch control lever.

As it doesn't isolate the battery it should not be used for normal switching off.

On machines which have an electric starter, the starter button will also be located on the throttle drum. Some Continental machines have their indicator switches (covered further on) on the right-hand side.

FRONT BRAKE, HYDRAULIC OR CABLE

The lever mounted on the right handlebar controls the front brake. If this is of the hydraulic type it will be self-adjusting but it will need occasional topping-up to the max line with the correct type of hydraulic fluid. The type to be used is normally stamped on the reservoir cover. Do not use fluid from an already open container, or old fluid (it is hygroscopic and absorbs moisture from the atmosphere which contaminates it and lowers its boiling point). Use fresh fluid only, clear of air bubbles (see below). Make sure there are no leaks or damage to the hydraulic hoses — which have to withstand very high pressures, several hundred p.s.i., under heavy braking. Don't spill brake fluid on paintwork or plastic as it will dissolve both quite cheerfully.

The brake lever works against a plunger or piston inside a cylinder — just like a small bicycle pump. The hydraulic pressure produced here when you pull on the lever is transmitted to similar, but larger diameter cylinders whose plungers push friction pads against the steel disc which is fixed to the front wheel. The plungers have a protective rubber boot, which keeps out dirt, and a rubber seal which acts like a weak spring, pulling the pads off the disc when the brake is released. The rubbers should be in good condition and you should learn (from the handbook or your dealer) how to inspect them and the friction pads for wear. Usually there is an inspection cover and the pads have a coloured portion — when they are worn down to the coloured marking they should be replaced. As the pads wear, the hydraulic pistons move further along the cylinders and more fluid is taken from the reservoir to fill the increased volume. Hence the brakes are self-adjusting, but the fluid level will gradually go down.

If air or vapour get into the hydraulic line your squeeze on the lever will merely tend to compress the gas instead of working the brake; the brake will feel "spongy" and will not be so powerful. The only cure is to pump the fluid — and gas — out through a bleed nipple, refilling with new fluid until the brake works properly. Get the exact details from the handbook, or have a dealer do it, but make sure that any brake defects are attended to *immediately.*

Air in the fluid can come from a leak or from wear in the cylinder/piston/sealing rubbers, or it can be dissolved in the fluid. For this reason, new containers should be left standing for as long as possible before opening and using the fluid. Vibration on the machine can cause frothing in the reservoir and if the fluid level is allowed to fall too low (there are marks on the reservoir) it can uncover the entry to the cylinder and let air in. Finally, the disc brake gets extremely hot and this heat can cause the fluid behind the pads to boil briefly, forming a bubble of its own vapour.

Many hydraulic brakes have an adjuster, in the form of a screw and locknut, so that the position the lever reaches when the brake begins to bite can be altered to suit your handspan. To adjust it slacken the locknut and turn the adjuster screw, pumping the lever a few times. When you have found the most comfortable position, hold the adjuster and tighten the locknut. Check that the brake lever cannot foul any part of the throttle or cable, even when squeezed very hard. (See Fig. 10, page 44.)

Cable operated brakes, both drum and disc, also have adjusters so that the lever position may be varied. All cables should be kept well oiled, and run in smooth loops so there are no tight corners even when the handlebars are turned or when the front forks are compressed. Inspect the steel inner cable regularly and renew it if there are any signs of fraying or broken strands. (See Fig. 8.)

Drum brakes, unlike the self-adjusting disc brakes, require regular adjustment to keep them at peak efficiency — check this carefully for your particular model and make sure the work is done as laid down.

SWITCHES AND WARNING LIGHTS AT CENTRE OF HANDLEBARS

Moving across to the centre of the handlebars there will be the key-operated ignition switch, warning lights and instruments. Some models have the lighting switch incorporated with the ignition, others have a separate switch on either left or right handlebar. Some later machines have a steering lock built into the ignition switch; others have a separate lock on the side of the steering head (the frame member immediately behind the headlamp).

Bikes will have some, or all, of the following warning lights: *Generator* (usually red). Lights up when ignition is switched on, goes out when the engine is running. If it does not go out, it means the generator is not charging the battery. On Italian bikes it is merely an ignition warning, and stays on all the time the ignition is switched on.

Oil pressure (colours vary). This light is controlled by a pressure-sensitive switch in the oil-feed. It lights up if the oil pressure falls below a critical point. After a cold start it may take a few seconds for the light to go out and it may flicker on while the engine is idling. If it comes on at any other time, stop immediately and check the cause. If there is oil in the engine and no obvious fault, have the lubrication system checked by a dealer.

Oil level. Bikes with separate oil tanks (especially two-strokes) may have a warning light which comes on when the tank is getting empty.

Neutral (usually green). This lights up to let the rider know the machine is not in gear.

Indicator (usually yellow). A repeater light for flashing indicators is required by law. The indicators, incidentally, must flash at a frequency of 60 to 120 times per minute.

Main beam (usually blue) comes on when the headlamp main beam is on. Some Italian bikes have another warning lamp for dipped beam as well. A few bikes have a tail-light warning which comes on with the brake light and flashes if the bulb fails.

INSTRUMENTATION

There are usually two instruments, a speedometer and a tachometer. The speedo registers the machine's road speed in mph and km/h and includes an odometer, recording the bike's total mileage, plus a resettable trip, which records individual journey distances. This can be quite useful as a fuel reminder, especially for bikes with small tanks, resetting it to zero whenever the tank is filled. Once you know how far the bike will go on a tankful, a glance at the trip meter will show how much fuel has been used.

The tachometer or rev counter shows the engine speed in revolutions per minute (rpm). At the high speed end there will be a red-coloured zone (yellow and then red on Italian bikes). This denotes the engine's safe speed limit; it is usually permissible to let the revs go into the red briefly during acceleration, but the engine should not be run at these speeds for any length of time.

The tacho has other uses as well: it is a help when making carburettor adjustments, particularly when correcting the idle speed and when setting the ignition timing. It will also help a first time rider to hold a steady engine speed while learning how to co-ordinate the clutch and throttle to pull away.

A few bikes have other instruments, such as a clock (very useful), voltmeter (useful, especially if you plan to use auxiliary lights and also for trouble-tracing) and fuel gauge (not very useful as accuracy is usually questionable). Instruments like these can be fitted as extras to pretty well any machine.

Others include: vacuum gauge (not recommended as single carburettor pulses are too strong and the bike's vibration tends to destroy the gauge — a good addition to a tool kit, though, for balancing multiple carburettors); ammeter — serves much the same purpose as a voltmeter, possibly not as versatile; temperature gauge (either coolant, oil or spark plug) — only really of value if you are doing development work; oil pressure gauge — of some value in giving warnings of impending doom.

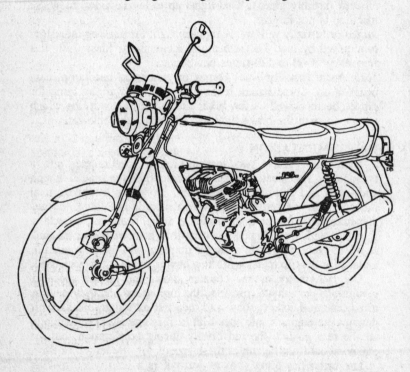

Fig. 7. Side view of typical machine. Note adjustable mirrors, indicators, passenger grab rail and fold-back footrests. The gear lever is positioned in front of the left footrest while the rear brake lever is on the right side of the machine out of view in this picture. The rear suspension is usually adjustable for spring pre-load (ride height) to compensate for varying loads. The fuel tap is located under the rear left of the fuel tank.

SWITCHES ON LEFT HANDLEBAR

There will be several switches on the left-hand grip:

Light switch — usually with three positions, OFF, PILOT and HEADLAMP. For riding, do not bother with the pilot or "sidelamp" — if you need to see ahead or if you want others to see you, use the headlamp. At night, or in poor visibility, you are legally required to use the headlamp *not* the pilot light.

Dipswitch — the headlamp bulb has two filaments. One gives a beam which is horizontal and gives you the best visibility. The other is set so that its beam is angled downwards and must be adjusted so that it does not dazzle oncoming drivers (or drivers in front of you via their mirrors). The Lighting Regulations stipulate dimensions; garages and dealers usually have beam-setters; in practice it is easy enough to stand in the road ahead of the bike, crouch to driver level and see how dazzling the light is.

Headlamp flasher — a spring-loaded switch (sometimes combined with the horn button) which flashes the headlamp's main beam. As a signal this can be a double-edged weapon; truck drivers, for example, might take a burst on the headlamp to mean "It is clear for you to pull in front of me" whereas you may have intended it to mean "beware I am coming through". In the *Highway Code* it says that the signal means the same as sounding the horn — it simply lets others know that you are there.

Horn button — an obvious warning sound — but it must not be used when the bike is in a built-up area between 11.30 p.m. and 7 a.m. or when it is not moving unless another vehicle on the move presents a threat.

Indicators — a three-position switch with OFF in the centre. Pushing to the right sets the right indicators flashing; to the left sets the left indicators flashing. After signalling, the switch has to be returned to the central position or pushed inwards to cancel the lights. Some manufacturers (Yamaha, BMW, Kawasaki) fit self-cancelling indicators which work on a time base, tripped by a disturbance sensor inside the speedo head. The signal is cancelled after the bike has travelled for (say) 50 metres and ten seconds.

CLUTCH

Lastly, on the left side of the handlebars there is a lever which operates the clutch, via a cable. The clutch can be visualised as two flat plates pushed together by springs like a sandwich with no filling. One is attached to the engine drive shaft and the other to the gearbox shafts and so to the back wheel. Pressed together under the force of the springs there is a continuous, solid drive to

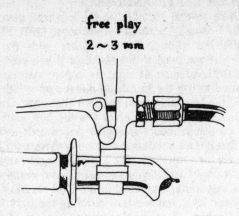

Fig. 8. The clutch cable adjuster should be used to make sure there is a couple of millimetres' free play in the cable. Cable brakes have a similar adjustment to control the lever position to suit your handspan.

the back wheel. The engine drive shaft turns one side of the "sandwich". The gearbox shaft is attached to the other and, since the two are clamped together by springs, finds itself turned in unison with the engine drive shaft. For starting off (and changing gear which is dealt with later) you squeeze the clutch lever and this intervenes and prises the plates apart, separating them against the spring pressure and so interrupting the drive. You can then engage first gear and, by easing the clutch control in smoothly (releasing the lever steadily) the plates can be brought back together slowly so that the speed of the driven plate (attached to wheel) slowly increases to the speed of the driving plate (from engine) and the bike will pull away steadily.

The clutch control lever should not have any tension in it when released otherwise it could hold the plates slightly apart and cause clutch *slip* while riding along. The cable adjuster should be set so that there is about 2mm or 3mm of free play before any strong resistance is felt. (See Fig. 8.)

FOOT CONTROLS

Moving away from the handlebars, there are foot controls on either side of the bike. On the right there is a brake pedal which operates the rear brake — and needs the same maintenance and adjustment as the front brake as discussed earlier (page 27). After adjusting, make sure any stoplight switch makes the light come on as soon as the pedal is moved.

On the left side there is the gear shift pedal. Have a look at Fig. 7. This may be adjustable on a splined shaft, or via a parallelogram linkage, so that it is a comfortable reach for your size of foot.

Most bikes have five or six gears, some have four; all, except for scooters and vintage bikes with hand gear levers, have what is known as a positive-stop shifter mechanism.

To select a gear, the pedal is pushed down or lifted up. This action slides a pair of meshed gear wheels along their shafts until they lock on to splines on the shafts or dogs (squared projections) on the sides of neighbouring gear wheels. That particular gear is then engaged. As the rider takes his foot off the pedal, it returns to its original central position, yet the ratchet-like mechanism stays put.

The next time the lever is moved, it slides the first pair of gear wheels out of engagement and pushes a second pair into engagement. And then returns to its mid-position.

THEORY OF GEAR RATIOS

Why have gears? Well, the engine's speed range isn't as wide as the range of speeds we need to use on the road. Take a bike which will run up to 9000rpm and has enough power to travel at 90mph. For top speed it will need to be geared to pull 10mph for every 1000rpm.

But at low speed it will, for example, only be turning at 2000rpm at 20mph; try to go slower and the engine will protest, jerking, snatching and spluttering because it cannot be made to run efficiently at these low speeds (at least not if we want it to give good power at 9000rpm). Even at 3000rpm it won't be giving much power and acceleration and the ability to climb hills will be poor.

So we incorporate a *lower* gear ratio. One that gives a speed of 30mph at our maximum of 9000rpm will take us down to 10mph at 3000. There is another big advantage: although we have reduced our road speed, we have increased torque − the thrust delivered to the back wheel.

This is because, in order to turn the back wheel the same distance, the engine now has to turn three times as far and is therefore putting thrice the effort into moving the bike. This is why you will feel much more response, much more pulling power, much better acceleration in a low gear − but it will not take you to such a high speed as a high gear.

In our example, one gear ratio was conveniently three times the other; on real engines the gear ratios are chosen to match the power characteristics and the desired road performance. A typical 100cc machine runs up to 8000rpm and would not normally be expected to run much below 2000rpm. Between these engine speeds its gears give the following speeds:

road speed mph	(Bottom) 1st gear rpm	2nd gear rpm	3rd gear rpm	4th gear rpm	(Top) 5th gear rpm
10	4000	2666	1600		
15					
20	8000	5333	3200	2909	2461
25					
30		8000	4800	4363	3692
35					
40					
45					
50			8000	7272	6153
55				8000	6769
60					
65					8000

This shows the equivalent engine speeds in each of the gears at various road speeds. For instance, at 20mph the rider could have the engine screaming at its 8000 maximum in 1st, at 5333rpm in 2nd, 3200 in 3rd, 2909 in 4th or 2461rpm in 5th (or top) gear.

This speed incidentally, is the only one where the rider could use any one of his five gears; any slower and the engine wouldn't pull properly in 5th − any faster and it would exceed its safe limit in 1st.

A chart like this also shows the "spacing" between the gears. There is, in this case, a big jump from 2nd to 3rd − the rider would find this the most difficult change to make smoothly. By comparison, 3rd and 4th gears are very close together; this would be the easiest, slickest change in the gearbox, as the engine would hardly know that anything had happened.

CHANGING GEAR

The chart shows what the rider has to do to make a gear change. A slow-motion replay of what the rider does would show us the following.

He is using 1st gear and accelerating quite briskly. The engine speed gets close to 8000rpm and his toe is already against the gear lever, pressing it lightly upwards. It doesn't move because the power being transmitted between the gear wheels holds them together.

As the engine reaches 8000rpm he quickly rolls the throttle off, not closing it down altogether, but moving it far enough to take the power out of the engine. This allows the gear selector mechanism to move; as he feels it give way he increases foot pressure and the gear lever moves rapidly. Just after rolling off the throttle but before the gear lever has moved, the rider swiftly pulls in the clutch lever, not all the way but just far enough to interrupt the drive.

The meshing gears are, just for an instant, in limbo, spinning but not being driven. First gear has been pushed out of mesh. The engine, deprived of its power, has lost speed rapidly. As the revs drop to 5400rpm, the spinning wheels which make second gear suddenly find they are travelling at nearly the same speed as the engine shaft. The gear shifter is now pushing them along a tiny distance towards splines on the shaft; at precisely 5333rpm of engine speed, the gears lock on to the spline. The rider feels it as a final click in the gear pedal. He is already releasing the clutch smoothly and increasing the throttle, taking up the drive and continuing the bike's acceleration.

The whole operation takes about 0.1 seconds. With a smooth gear shift it is not always necessary to use the clutch, but unless the engine revs are matched perfectly to the new gear, there will be jerkiness and this will be emphasised if the clutch isn't used.

Of course the rider doesn't have to go up to the engine's rev limit. He could change up earlier; at 10mph he would have 4000rpm and would have to drop the engine speed to 2666rpm for second gear.

Similarly, at 30mph he could be running 4800rpm in 3rd, 4363 in 4th or 3692 in 5th gear.

On most machines the gear lever is pushed upwards to change

up into a higher gear. Pushing it downwards selects a lower gear, although there are one or two machines in which this sequence is reversed.

Changing down is probably a little more difficult to co-ordinate. Let's say our rider is travelling at something like 50mph in top gear and wants to slow down steadily. He shuts the throttle and maybe brakes lightly. The bike slows down and at 30mph it is turning at 3692rpm. The rider pushes down on the gear lever, eases the clutch lever in and, as he feels the gear disengage, "blips" the throttle. (He opens the twistgrip slightly, just enough to speed the engine up and immediately shuts off again). The engine revs soar up to just over 4000, and the rider still has foot pressure bearing down on the pedal. At 4363rpm, 4th gear engages. The rider eases the lever out and lets the clutch engage.

Naturally the rider doesn't try to remember precise rpm figures − he remembers the feel of the bike, whether it is a large or small jump between particular gears and whether to give the throttle a big blip or a small blip.

ENGINE BRAKING

When the throttle is closed for deceleration, the engine behaves like a pump being driven by the back wheel and its resistance helps slow the bike down. This engine braking effect is obviously greater in a lower gear because the wheel will have to turn the engine more times at any particular road speed.

If the rider misjudges the revs to match the gear change the bike will protest accordingly. If he gives it too much speed, it will surge forward as the gear engages; if he gives it too little speed, the sudden braking effect will slow the bike violently, just for a split second, maybe making the back wheel lock momentarily. (The wheel stops turning and slides, which can be dangerous especially if aggravated by a poor road surface.)

Obviously smooth, well-judged gear changes give a much more comfortable ride, as well as causing less wear and tear on the machinery.

Engine braking is a useful mode of control on steep downhills and in slippery conditions.

GEARS FOR CLIMBING HILLS

Using a lower gear has two effects; it increases the engine's thrust on the bike and it reduces the speed at which the engine can propel the bike. This extra thrust can be used in a variety of ways − for extra urge to overtake things, or to hold speed against a steep climb or a strong headwind. On smaller, low-powered machines it often becomes something of an art to choose the optimum gear to get up hills or to maintain the highest speed over a difficult section of road. As learners are restricted to low-powered machines it is worthwhile exploring these different possibilities and getting as familiar as possible with the various combinations of engine speed and gear ratio until the machine can always be ridden in the right gear without the rider having to give it a second thought.

4
Using the Controls

Understanding the various controls and how they work helps a rider to visualise what is happening mechanically and to develop a sympathetic method of using the controls. It makes things easier if they are kept in good adjustment and slick working order. Regular checks should be made whenever the bike is ridden, on basic safety items. Make a rule to check the tyre pressures, brake light, indicators, horn, both brakes, fuel and oil levels. Most of this can be done while you are fastening your helmet, switching on the fuel and ignition and checking that the gearshift is in neutral. And whenever the bike is cleaned, say once a week, a more thorough check should be made.

FAMILIARISE YOURSELF WITH THE BRAKES

Before your first ride (at a suitable spot, see page 24), it is essential to familiarise yourself with the position of the brake levers and to get used to the "feel" of the brakes. Push the machine forward against brake pressure; roll it along and stop it with the brakes.

Braking technique is covered in detail later on. As it is vital to know how to stop the bike before practising any riding, you should be fully conversant with all of the operations before setting out on the bike – even on private ground. If things start to go wrong on the first practice rides, pull in the clutch and gently brake the machine to a standstill.

STARTING UP

From a cold start the bike will need the choke (or cold start lever) and will need to be run for a few seconds until the engine responds predictably to the throttle. While starting use the starter motor in short bursts and not in a long grind which will only flatten the battery. If the machine has a kick-start, push it gently, turning the engine until you feel the extra resistance of the compression stroke. Ease it past compression, then let the kick-start pedal return to the top of the stroke and give a full, fast swing. This will turn the engine furthest and fastest and give the best chance of firing up.

In both cases keep the throttle either closed or just slightly open, opening it further as you feel the engine fire and start to pick up. Push the cold start lever off as soon as possible.

It is a good idea to get into the habit of doing all the preliminary things in the same sequence; making the various checks, switching the motor on, etc. On the rare occasions that something is wrong, you will stand more chance of noticing it and, on the odd time when you are a bit forgetful or concentrating on other things, it may save you the embarrassment of riding away with the petrol switched off or, worse still, with the prop stand down. Since the late '80s, bikes have been fitted with various devices to prevent this, often in the form of a lock-out switch which cuts the ignition if you attempt to ride away with the stand down.

BIKE CHECK-OUT

Once a week, or at a convenient time like when you wash the bike down, carry out the more detailed checks. You will find that specific items for individual machines are listed in their service handbooks, but typically they include a complete check of all the controls, oiling or greasing exposed and moving parts and also checking the tyres, not only for pressure but for sidewall damage, wear on the treads and for stones etc., trapped in the tread, needing removal.

When a tyre's tread depth goes down to 2 or 3mm, the handling goes off noticeably. Steering on wet roads is less precise and the machine reacts when it crosses raised lines in the road by twitching rapidly from side to side. The tyres should be changed at this point, even though the minimum legal tread depth is only 1.6mm.

Continuing with the check-up, you should test for play in the steering and suspension, check spoke tension in the wheels (by tapping them − tight spokes will give a clear, ringing note) and chain tension. The chain will probably need lubricating as well. All of the electrical items should be checked, along with the level of electrolyte in the battery. This should be topped up to the level marks with distilled water, if necessary. Some machines have sealed-for-life batteries which need no maintenance.

Check brake pads for wear, engine and gearbox oil levels and finally look for loose nuts and bolts around the bike.

Again, most of this can be done as you clean each part of the bike, so it needn't be as tedious as it sounds.

WARMING UP

Riding the bike well depends on practice, with smooth, easy co-ordination as the target. After starting the engine it will warm up fastest on a light load, being ridden slowly for a mile or so before giving the engine any real work to do. Cold running is the biggest enemy of all engines. With the choke on they run too rich and neat petrol can wash oil from the cylinder walls; the oil itself is too thick and doesn't flow properly to give good lubrication; it develops high pressures which can easily damage oil seals; the rather acidic by-products of combustion condense as a liquid where they can contaminate the oil, or slowly attack metals — such as the inside of the exhaust. So it's in your interest to warm the engine as quickly as possible and not to make it rev hard until it is up to full working temperature.

Throttle response is also poor, especially if the engine is cold enough to depend on the choke control. For this reason it is better for a novice rider to let it warm up before trying to ride, by holding the throttle slightly open so that the motor idles for a while at a steady 3000rpm. If a rev counter isn't fitted, this sounds like a very fast tick-over, but not so fast that the engine sounds as if it is "racing".

HOW TO START OFF FROM REST

Initial pulling away calls for the same slight degree of throttle movement. With the engine idling normally (throttle closed), pull in the clutch lever and push down on the gear pedal to engage 1st gear. This will be selected more easily if the engine is turning slowly. (If the gear still isn't happy about it, try rocking the bike backwards and forward a little. This movement of the back wheel should turn the gear wheels enough via the chain to make the splines, etc. line up.)

Ease the throttle open to a fast idle — around 2000rpm — and, as you don't want to pull off with your eyes glued to the rev-counter, remember what this sounds like.

What you have to do next is to ease the clutch home by letting the lever move smoothly and steadily away from the handlebar. As the clutch grips, it will nudge the whole bike forward and the revs will drop as the load slows the engine down. Don't let this take you by surprise and jerk your body backwards, otherwise you will either shut the throttle and stall the motor, or inadvertently open the throttle and make a noisy and possibly spectacular leap forward.

After a bit of practice you will learn how far the clutch lever moves before it takes up the drive. At this point it helps if you can lean forward slightly and let most of your weight be taken through the seat. You only need the tips of your toes on the road for balance and the less weight there is on them, the less chance you have of being left standing in the road when the bike decides it's time to go.

With what weight there is on your feet it might help just to push the bike forward — but restrict it to one push and concentrate on getting your feet on the footrests as quickly as possible. Avoid paddling off down the road with both legs flailing away — it only upsets your balance and steering control. And remember, LOOK AHEAD.

As the clutch bites and the engine tries to slow down, you must open the throttle a little more — but only just enough to compensate and keep the engine speed steady — and then let the clutch lever out a little further. This progressive co-ordination is the thing that most learners find the most difficult. The key is the engine speed — it must be high enough to prevent the motor stalling yet not so high that the bike scorches off like a Santa Pod dragster.

Using the throttle to maintain a steady engine speed can only be mastered by practice. In fact the more slowly you try to do it, the more difficult it becomes because the clutch and throttle are harder to equalise and the bike itself is quite difficult to balance when it is moving at extremely low speeds. Unfortunately the first few attempts will have to be fairly slow … Remember if you get worried at any stage you can always stop, as explained at the start of this chapter.

Aim to get the clutch fully home as quickly as possible, consistent with a smooth take-off and only use the minimum amount of throttle until the clutch is home. After that, adjust speed on the throttle and try to ride along without touching the clutch at all until you want to stop or change gear.

When you have mastered this (on a private, practice area, and obtained your Compulsory Basic Training certificate) you will have to go through the same steps on public roads except now you need to take a good look behind first. Make sure the road is clear for long enough to allow time to pull away and get up to speed. If you have to hesitate for any reason, stop, check behind and start again. You should use the right indicator to show that you are about to leave the kerbside and join the traffic flow, but in the early stages it is more important that you make sure there is nobody behind you to see it.

Part of the test involves pulling away from behind a parked car; that is, turning at an angle from the kerbside and moving out smoothly into the road while making sure there is no traffic coming up from behind, and no other road users (pedestrians crossing, an overtaking vehicle coming from the opposite direction, etc.) who might be intent on using the same piece of road.

A problem that learners suffer in the early stages is that, having checked behind, they then take so long to get the revs and clutch co-ordination right that the traffic situation has changed completely. They are oblivious to this — in their concentration they haven't realised just how long it has taken — and therefore it is very difficult to prevent. Just be aware that the problem exists; if in doubt, abort the start, take a good look all round and try again. The whole point of your CBT (Compulsory Basic Training) is that you should be able to make essential manoeuvres like this with confidence and no delay. If there is a problem, practise on private ground until you feel competent.

STOPPING

The next thing is to learn rather more about how to stop! Safe use of the brakes is so important we will return to the subject in detail later — page 50. The only likely difficulty at this stage is in reaching the controls quickly and in squeezing the control without grabbing it (or, for the rear brake, pressing steadily instead of stamping on the pedal). It is a matter of practice to acquire the familiarity with the controls to know just where they will begin to bite and how much pressure will have how much effect so that you don't overdo things. At these low speeds it is quite easy to lock the wheels, especially on loose or wet surfaces. Don't pull in the clutch at once with the brake — a method only appropriate to the first ever half hour or so in the saddle. For normal stopping you pull the clutch in during the last second or two before the machine comes to a standstill so the engine does not stall.

If you are going to stop for more than a few seconds (and this will apply later in traffic) select "neutral". This is between 1st and 2nd gears and is located by lifting the pedal slightly so that 1st gear disengages but not so far that 2nd is engaged. This will avoid damage caused by overheating the clutch.

By the nature of the gear selector mechanism, it is usually easier to find neutral while the wheels are still turning; therefore most experienced riders push the gear selector to neutral when they pull in the clutch as the bike rolls to a stop.

CHANGING GEARS

Once you can start and stop successfully, you can begin changing gears. You may have found the throttle response in 1st gear somewhat jerky anyway and learning to ride the bike at low speed becomes easier once you can get up into 2nd gear. This is because the torque multiplication and therefore the throttle response and acceleration is far greater in the lowest gears. It is easier to control the bike in higher gears because any lack of perfection in throttle control will not cause such an immediate and violent response from the bike.

If you practise these initial starts and stops on an off-road training area there may only be room to get up into 3rd or even 2nd gear. Nevertheless you should discover how much it helps to pull the highest gear possible, without making the engine judder or labour too strongly. The sequence for changing gear was explained at the end of Chapter 3.

Fig. 9. Manoeuvring or stopping across slopes. Position the bike so that you put down the foot (or get off the bike) on the uphill side. To manoeuvre, turn it up the slope, so that it can be held on the brakes and the engine used to drive it uphill, and if it is necessary to roll it backwards, gravity will do that for you while you check the bike with the brakes. To park, turn so that the propstand is on the downhill side, and roll the bike back until the rear wheel rests against a kerb, etc.

EXTRA SLOW RIDING TECHNIQUE

When riding slowly and wanting to drop to a crawl, ignore the clutch until the engine is turning so slowly in 1st gear that it is in danger of snatching and jerking. Then, if you need to go still more slowly, ease the clutch in just far enough to free the engine so it cannot stall. At this point, delicately open the throttle as though for pulling away and slowly feed the clutch out and in, letting it bite and slip so as to keep the bike moving at the slow pace you require. Check the bike's speed by lightly touching one of the brakes.

STOPPING ON A SLOPE/HILL START

Where there is a slope or if a road is steeply cambered it is necessary to hold the bike from running back after it has stopped rolling. See Fig. 9. The best procedure is to hold it on the front brake, keeping the right foot on the floor and using the left foot to select 1st gear. Then, if you can control both the front brake and

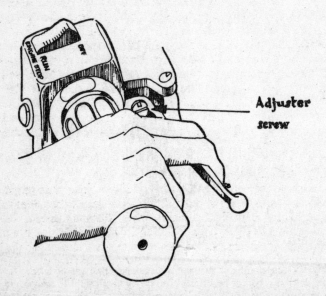

Adjuster screw

Fig. 10. Operating the brake in this manner lets the rider control the throttle easily as well — but make sure that the lever cannot trap the fingers. The adjuster screw controls the position of the lever relative to when the brake begins to "bite" on hydraulic systems. See Fig. 8 for cable adjusters.

the throttle (see Fig. 10), ease the brake off as you feed in the clutch to take the load off the bike.

If you cannot manage this, select the gear and then put your left foot down to balance the bike. Use your right foot to hold the back brake on and prevent the bike rolling back with the slope. As the clutch takes up the drive, slowly let the brake off. Unless you have perfect co-ordination, the engine will be driving against the brake (slightly) as well as the slope and so you will need to use rather more power than for a normal take-off on level ground.

It is worth getting into the habit of using the brakes before pulling away, even if it isn't strictly necessary to prevent the bike rolling forward or back before you are ready. It stops you being fooled by a slope which looks flat and it encourages proper co-ordination. On a downhill slope it prevents you acquiring the bad practice of having your wheels rolling before a gear is engaged — the bike would be coasting and not under proper control — examiners would take a dim view.

Although it is kind to the clutch to select neutral when stopping, and on most machines it is easier to select neutral just before the wheels stop rolling, there is one time when you should be very careful about taking the machine out of gear.

This is if the machine has drum brakes and if you have to stop on a very steep upward slope. The reason is that twin-leading shoe brakes do not work very well in reverse: the front brake will not prevent the machine rolling back down a steep slope. The rear brake, being a single leading shoe, will be able to hold it. But having one foot on the brake doesn't leave any spare feet for selecting gears! The only answer calls for some very rapid and ungainly antics ...

LOW SPEED MANOEUVRES

Mastery of your bike at low speeds is your next target and ironically this is one of the most difficult skills to develop; at low speeds the motorcycle doesn't have the momentum or the castoring effect (see page 59) from its steering to give it a lot of stability. The handlebars seem almost too easy to turn and the bike will follow, wherever you point it. Very smooth throttle control is a big help, avoiding any sudden change in speed.

If you have room to do it away from the roads, it helps to mark out a course with figure-8 and slalom sections to follow. See Fig. 4 in Chapter 1. The tighter the turns the more difficult it will be to manoeuvre. When you can do so at a steady speed, try accelerating gently through the easier parts and slowing for the

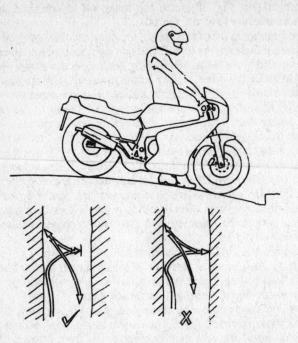

Fig. 11. To turn the bike in a confined space, plan the manoeuvre so that the terrain helps rather than hinders. Typically, a narrow road might have quite a steep camber, so turn across the road (steering right in these diagrams) but stop on the crown before the front goes down the camber into the gutter. Then the bike may be rolled backwards down the camber (steering left). It can now be ridden under its own power, up the camber (steering right) to complete the turn. Choose a place where there is enough visibility in both directions, so that the turn can be completed without hindering other traffic.

more difficult bits. Change up and down between, say 2nd and 3rd, and even 1st, gears. *And all the time watch out for anyone else who might be using the same ground, for example on foot.*

At these low speeds the motorcycle steers like most other vehicles, by turning its front wheel in the direction you want it to go. The radius of the turn is proportional to the angle the wheel turns through.

Should you need to dismount your bike to turn it round in a very narrow area, see Fig. 11. There can be snags if you need to ride across a step or a gutter! See Fig. 12.

Fig. 12. Think out all manoeuvres first. Be particularly careful if you have to cross slopes, steps, kerbs, etc., because this can change the effective ground clearance considerably, making it difficult to reach the floor and keep balance if you have to stop.

WEIGHT DISTRIBUTION

It is necessary for the rider to keep his balance and, to some extent the slower he goes, the more difficult it becomes. You will quickly find that the riding position makes a big difference to the ease of control. Don't hold on to the handlebars too tightly, keep a relaxed grip but steer firmly and positively. Use all of the controls smoothly; sudden movements make the bike respond with a jerk which tries to snatch the controls from your hands and as you grab back it often flicks the controls even harder, making the bike move more violently still.

Sit forward, so that your feet are below, or preferably slightly behind your body weight and take a fair portion of your weight through the footrests. This will allow you to feel the machine twisting below you and to sense changes of direction more easily.

Try not to put your feet down, but if you have to, do it fairly slowly, reaching *forwards* and outwards with your foot and taking more of your weight on the other foot, which is still on the footrest. Using a foot for balancing should be no more than a gentle push to bring the bike upright — don't try and stand on that foot because you are still moving forwards and, relative to you, the ground is moving backwards. Put any weight on the groundside foot and the floor will grip and soon pull it beyond the back of the bike, which is great fun for spectators.

From this basic riding position you can even try standing on the footrests — you might find that this helps to balance while you are making very tight turns. Try also the effects of shifting your body weight, from side to side, and backwards and forwards. Certain positions can help low-speed steering.

Normally it is better to shift body weight so that as the bike turns and leans slightly, you keep your body vertical, and let the bike move beneath you. Take most of your weight through the footrest on the outside of the turn. If you have to stop, or if the bike overbalances, or a wheel slips on loose gravel, it will then be easy to put the inside foot down for support. As the bike will already be leaning to the inside of the turn, if it does slip or topple, that is the way it will go.

Weight distribution does make a large difference to manoeuvrability — but in the end, whatever feels most comfortable is the best for you.

FIRST TIME ON THE ROAD

At this point, unless you have a large training ground, you won't be able to learn a lot more without going out onto the road. However, until you are happy that you can control your machine comfortably you will be well advised not to take to the road.

Before your first run on the road read through Chapter 5 on braking and you will need a reasonable understanding of the rules of the road as set out in the *Highway Code* — which is the whole purpose of Compulsory Basic Training.

A quiet country lane devoid of traffic makes a fairly attractive starting point. Even on deserted lanes, though, you now have the prospect of much faster traffic coming not only from ahead, but also from behind. As a matter of self defence you need to make a habit of looking behind very frequently. Use the mirrors by all means, but look over your shoulder as well, especially until you know how much field of view the mirrors give. *The test requires that you look round before stopping, overtaking, turning or beginning any manoeuvre affecting other traffic.* So learn well.

For general riding aim to use about one-quarter throttle or a shade more and to keep the engine speed somewhere in the middle range. Accelerate to, say, 4000rpm and then change up until you are cruising in top gear at 35mph to 40mph; if that seems unduly fast (and it probably will on your first trip) don't be worried about slowing down to a speed at which you feel in control.

The rule of the road is drive on the left. Therefore keep well away from the middle of the road. However, too near the kerb tends to be bumpy and debris collect, so you should strike a balance between too far out and too close in. Later, for multi-lane roads, see page 110.

Use the gears; if you have to slow down, change down a gear when the revs drop to 3000 − so despite the lower speed you keep the engine spinning between 3000 and 4000rpm. Maintain it in that range by changing up or down through the gears as necessary when you need to alter speed.

You will have to start looking out for obstacles well ahead now, so that you can react to them with plenty of time and won't have to make any sudden, last-minute moves. To prepare your reactions we return to a more sophisticated look at braking in the next chapter.

At this stage it is important to continue to practise stopping, starting and gear shifts, gaining confidence, co-ordination and the feel of the controls. It sometimes helps to do this in a small group; that way you can learn from others' mistakes and it teaches you to watch out for other vehicles while you are riding.

BE SYSTEMATIC

Once under way on public roads, try to get into the habit of making regular sweeps with the eyes; road − mirrors − speedo − warning lights − road. It only takes a second, maybe less, and if you follow the same sequence it lessens the chance of missing something when you are suddenly thrown into an unfamiliar or frightening situation. It should also stop you leaving an indicator flashing after its use is over − one of the most dangerous oversights.

5
Braking

As a general principle, always try to brake as gently as possible, using both brakes together, and do all the braking while the bike is travelling in a straight line, before it gets to a corner.

It is important first of all, however, to learn the feel of each brake before using them together, and well before a need might arise to use both to brake hard.

STOPPING PRACTICE FROM LOW SPEED

For these initial stops make sure the road is dry and has a good surface, free of loose gravel, etc. Practise each brake, individually, lightly, concentrating on the feel or the feedback you get from the control itself and from the bike in general — weight transfer, suspension movement and so on. You don't have to think of it in technical terms as long as you can physically feel what's going on. Then progress to using both together to get the feel of how you will normally use your brakes. Don't get into the habit of relying on just one of them; you must use them both together until you can do it automatically. The reason for this will be explained under emergency stopping below.

Next — well away from anyone who might run into the back of you — practise measured stops from a steady but modest speed, using just the front brake, then the back brake and then both brakes. Distances always look different when you go back and pace them out and you are likely to find some surprising differences between the braking capabilities.

STOPPING FROM HIGHER SPEED

For your future safety it is worth finding out how efficient your brakes are from higher speed, as long as you do it well away from other traffic. An additional technique at the handlebar may now be adopted.

While using the front brake, you will often find that you need fingers around the handlebar, to help steering, or to change down through the gears as you slow down. Most modern brakes need quite a light force and using just the first two fingers on the brake

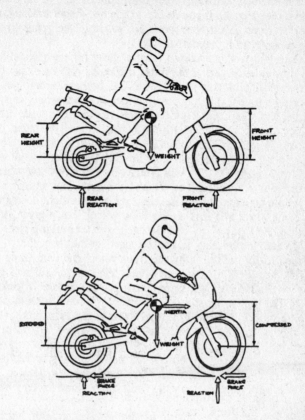

Fig. 13. The amount of braking force a tyre can give depends on its grip (the friction between it and the road surface) and on the load carried by that wheel. The braking force is generated between the tyre and the road, i.e. at ground level, while the inertia and the weight of the bike act through its centre of gravity, somewhere near the middle of the bike. When the bike is standing still or being ridden at a steady speed, its weight is shared fairly equally between front and rear wheels, so both have roughly equal grip. During braking, the rearward acting brake force and the bike's inertia, acting higher up, set up a twisting force that tries to rotate the bike forwards, clockwise in these drawings. This is called weight transfer. It compresses the front suspension and extends the rear suspension; more weight is carried on the front wheel, less on the rear. Consequently, the front tyre has much more grip than the rear and can provide much more braking force.

lever is enough. Whatever feels most comfortable is the best way to do it. See Fig. 10. If you decide to use two-finger braking, make sure the lever adjustment won't let you trap the remaining two fingers against the handlebar.

When you first try to stop from slightly higher speeds, notice how it suddenly gets a lot more difficult. As you react to the greater difficulty and start to use the brakes harder, you will probably notice that it gets easier to lock the back wheel so it stops turning and slides. On a good surface, though, it is quite difficult to lock the front wheel, which is just as well because if you succeed in making this wheel slide, you will probably fall off.

The front wheel can give more braking effort because of weight transfer. See Fig. 13. You will already have noticed that when you brake, your body weight is pitched forward. This inertia affects the whole bike and during deceleration more weight is carried on the front wheel and less on the back wheel. For a given level of friction, the front wheel can tolerate a greater braking force. And the greater the braking force, the more weight transfer.

In typically hard braking the front wheel can contribute 80%, leaving just 20% for the rear wheel. The rear wheel will accept only one-quarter of the front braking force before it locks and skids. The higher the speed from which you are having to slow or stop, the more difficult it becomes to use the rear brake without the risk of locking the back wheel and making it skid or start hopping. The use of sports (or soft compound) tyres means that the front wheel can generate even more braking force, leaving even less weight on the rear wheel and, for this reason, many experienced riders use only the front brake when braking hard on a good surface.

It is important to be able to use both brakes though, because if you have to brake on a wet surface, or when the bike is leaning into a turn, you cannot use as much front brake and then the ability to control the rear brake is crucial.

If there is a risk of the front wheel locking, it helps to shift your weight forward by moving forward in the seat and by sitting upright. This is because anything that raises or moves forward the bike's centre-of-gravity will shift more weight to the front wheel during braking and will give it more traction.

When the bike is banked over, a certain amount of tyre grip is used up in producing the cornering force. Therefore there is less grip available for braking (or for acceleration, for that matter). If you have to brake, you need to do it smoothly and gently, if possible lifting the bike slightly (bringing it more upright) to reduce the cornering force and make more grip available for braking.

Some years ago, when tyres and suspension were at a basic level, riders were taught to do all their braking in a straight line. The density of traffic since then has changed that, but fortunately, tyres and chassis have changed as well. As they developed, the wisdom was that you could use the back brake, *gently*, to scrub off speed in a turn, mainly on the grounds that if the back wheel skidded it was relatively easy to control and the brake could be released before the bike went out of control. On the other hand if the front wheel locked, the machine tended to crash very quickly. Now, tyres (and frame stiffness and suspension control, but mostly tyres) have improved further and it is possible to use a fair amount of front brake while cornering. Obviously it has to be done with a great amount of care and can be balanced by delicate use of the back brake too. The effect of braking force and suspension movement (due to weight transfer) also change the steering geometry. Depending on the individual bike's settings, this can vary from no perceptible change through to a strong tendency for the bike to straighten up. This reaction can be altered by adjusting the rear damper settings, changing the front or rear ride height (or spring pre-load) and by changing the type of tyre and its pressure (assuming that such adjustments are available). The effect can only be found by experiment but as a general guide, the tendency to sit up on the brakes can be reduced by increasing the rear rebound damping, increasing the rear spring pre-load or ride height, or reducing the front spring pre-load or ride height.

EMERGENCY STOPPING

You will get maximum braking for an emergency stop using both brakes just short of the point where the wheels lock or where the rear wheel lifts off the floor. A locked wheel generates far less friction than one which is rolling, so if a wheel locks up, the bike will travel much further before stopping. At this level of braking you will need to pull in the clutch as soon as the speed drops below 30mph, in order to keep the engine running and to prevent a stalled engine locking the back wheel (see page 36).

It follows from the locking problem that for normal stopping, as for emergency, it is far better to put the brakes on progressively, rather than banging them straight up to full power — this gives you the chance to feel what is happening and to balance the level of front-to-rear braking so as not to lock a wheel at any stage. The need to be able to sense the effects on the bike is why there has been so much emphasis in this chapter on your acquiring a "feel" for using your brakes skilfully.

As you brake, it is a good idea to shift down through the gears — although there may not be time in an emergency — since this will leave you in the optimum gear for subsequent acceleration. However, lower gears give more engine braking and this can often exceed the rear wheel's adhesion limit, especially if the gear change is made raggedly, insufficiently co-ordinated with the reducing road speed. The result usually makes the back wheel hop in a series of short, sharp jumps and the way to avoid it is to use less braking force and to match the gear change revs smoothly.

Ideally it is best to use both brakes together and to brake while the machine is travelling in a straight line. Not all emergencies, regrettably, fit in with this ideal! On slippery surfaces, or when the bike is leaning over in a corner, it may still be necessary to slow down, in which case you are probably best to use more rear brake as cautiously as possible, at least initially. If the rear wheel skids, you stand a fair chance of controlling the bike whereas a front wheel slide almost certainly means a crash.

EVASIVE ACTION BRAKING AND LAST RESORTS

If there is a suitable training ground, it is worth experimenting with locked rear wheels, at low speeds, so that at least you know what it feels like. One day what you learn about evasive action could save your skin. A loose or slippery surface makes it easier, and causes less tyre wear, too. Ride in a straight line at 10mph or 15mph. Pull in the clutch and put the back brake on, progessively until it locks the wheel. Keep steering straight ahead: if the bike slides out to one side, keep steering where you want to go and keep the back brake on until you come to a stop. If the bike gets crossed up, don't let the brake off because the wheel may suddenly grip and flick the bike back into the straight-ahead position so quickly that you will be thrown out of the seat. This is called "high-siding" and it is to be avoided! It is unlikely to happen at these low speeds but it is as well to be aware of the possibility.

If there is too much grip and it is not easy to lock the rear wheel, use a little front brake — the weight transfer will make it easier to lock up the back wheel. Having slithered to a standstill in a straight line, and got the feel of the bike in this condition, repeat the exercise at the same speed but this time turn the handlebar slightly to the left as soon as the rear wheel locks. The whole bike will turn to the left and will keep turning as long as you keep steering that way.

At low speeds the bike will come to a standstill before it turns very far, but it is possible to turn it right round. A left turn is recommended because you'll have your right foot on the brake pedal, making the left one more convenient for extra balance, should you need it.

This manoeuvre can turn the bike around — at low speeds — or it is possible to turn it completely sideways to its direction of travel and lay it down. This is called "low-siding" and is a last resort when all other evasive action has been used up. It is preferable to hitting something and much better than high-siding because you are left behind the bike. However, if you're put in a position where you decide such a radical step is the only alternative, it must be done decisively, even forcefully. A half-hearted attempt will not work and if you get half-way through the manoeuvre and then let the brakes off, there's a fair chance that the bike will high-side you and you'll be worse off than ever because you'll hit whatever's in the way and then the bike will hit you. Laying the bike down is a deliberate attempt to reverse this sequence of events.

At low speeds — 20mph or less — hard braking is usually the best evasive action, because you can stop so quickly, even on a poor surface. At higher speeds you have to make a bigger and bigger choice between steering and braking, or even accelerating.

The problem is that it's hard to do both — swerve and brake — and it is important to recognise these limitations. *The neatest solution is to develop riding habits which don't get you into this kind of position.*

6
High Speed Control

Having become adept at low-speed manoeuvres and co-ordination, the next step is to handle the machine at higher speeds. "High speed", as far as the motorcycle is concerned, means anything over 20mph. From this speed upwards there is a marked difference in the way the bike responds.

Below this region the machine can be stopped very quickly and easily; at higher speeds braking distances become vastly longer and the degree of judgment and anticipation has to be increased in proportion.

STOPPING DISTANCES

In theory the stopping distance varies as the square of the bike's speed. On a good surface a machine should be able to stop in 10 metres, or less, from 30mph; the same bike should therefore be able to stop in 40 metres from 60mph — in theory. In practice it takes further, partly because the rider is unwilling to apply maximum brake pressure immediately at higher speeds and partly because any lag in the controls will let the bike travel further before anything happens.

The *Highway Code* applies this speed-squared law and adds a constant time factor for the rider's reaction. Its authors have chosen a reaction time of 0.68 seconds — which originally gave a "thinking distance" of 1 foot for every mph of speed, e.g. 60 feet at 60mph (which has now been converted to 18 metres (59 feet)). Typical braking distances are based on a 14 metre stop from 30mph, something which all motorcycles should be able to better, but in an unexpected traffic situation their figures are probably quite reasonable. The point is that the distances increase enormously as speed goes up, and, in poor conditions, the stopping distances increase alarmingly. It is extremely difficult to find and use maximum braking on a slippery surface so there is little point in trying to quote typical distances other than to say the "dry" distance could be more than doubled in the wet.

The distances (96 metres, or roughly the length of a football field at 70mph) are already becoming academic. Without positive reference points it is quite difficult to estimate this sort of distance; after a fair amount of experience under difficult conditions you will get a "feel" for the distance involved. However, it is probably true to say that most riders over-estimate their braking capabilities, thinking that they have more in reserve when they are, in fact, very close to the limit.

So, if you can find somewhere safe to do it, it is very instructive to experiment with braking distances from various speeds. Use markers and pace out the distance — you'll be surprised how far it takes to stop once you have to walk it! Compare the stopping distances for front brake alone, rear brake alone, rear brake — still alone but skidding — and both brakes together. Even at 30mph the differences will be surprising.

And this can be compared with the 3-6 metres or so in which a bike can stop from 20mph.

STEERING

Another barrier is broken in the 15-20mph region, this time to do with steering. At lower speeds the handlebars have to be turned in the direction you wish the bike to go and the radius of the turn depends on the amount the 'bars are turned. At higher speeds, as you will have observed other motorcyclists doing, you have to lean in to the bend. There is little appreciable movement of the handlebars but, to help make the machine lean over against centrifugal force, the rider in fact has to apply a small *opposite* force to the handlebar. To lean to the right, for example, it is necessary to apply some left torque to the handlebar, to exert a degree of pull trying to turn the handlebars to the left.

There are two factors which explain this. One is the gyroscopic behaviour of the front wheel (which, at speed, makes a very powerful gyroscope). In this, a phenomenon called precession makes a gyroscope turn in a plane at right-angles to the force which is trying to move it. As far as the front wheel is concerned at higher speeds, a force which tries to *turn* the handlebars to the left will cause the wheel to *lean* to the right. And vice versa; a turning force to the right produces a leaning movement to the left. (If you want to see for yourself, borrow a bicycle wheel and hold it by the spindle with the wheel spinning. Now try and steer it in a particular direction.) In the example above the slight pressure on the handlebars to the left (in apparently the wrong direction) thus aids in leaning the bike to the right.

In addition to the gyroscopic force, there is centrifugal force. If, when a machine is travelling along, the front wheel is turned

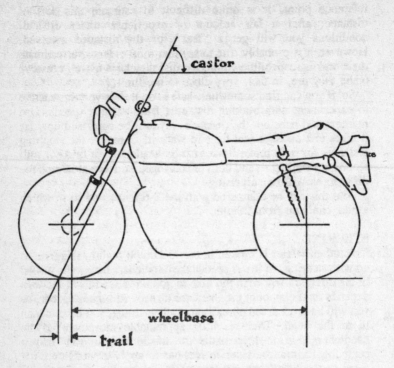

Fig. 14. The important factors in a machine's steering geometry.

slightly to the left, the machine will tend to steer to the left. This left-turning force is generated where the tyres meet the road. The bike's inertia, or its desire to continue straight-line motion, shows up in the form of a "centrifugal" reaction towards the outside of the slight turn being steered. This reaction force acts to the right and acts through the machine's centre of gravity — which is roughly level with the tops of the wheels.

So, the instant the rider exerts a mild left-turn force on the handlebar two forces are generated on the bike, the turning force at road level to the left and the centrifugal reaction at knee-height to the right. The latter makes the bike lean to the right and, as it pivots at road level, this will happen regardless of the first force. In consequence, because of centrifugal force, a slight left-turn at the handlebar has the immediate effect of making the machine lean to the right.

We now have two modes of control. At higher speed, pulling the handlebar just a little to the left causes the machine to lean to the right. As you will see later, the pull is not enough to turn the handlebar an appreciable amount. At very low speed, turning the handlebar left, turns the front wheel left and the bike actually steers in that direction. (Because of the low speed, centrifugal force which is trying to overturn the bike is not great and, in fact, is countered by the machine's steering geometry.)

STEERING GEOMETRY

Fig. 14 shows how the steering axis is angled (castor or rake) and how the tyre's contact patch follows behind this axis (trail). This arrangement, plus its relationship to the wheelbase and the centre of gravity of the machine, is crucial to its stability and its controllability. The centre of gravity − the point about which the whole of the bike's mass is balanced − also has to include the mass of the rider. Obviously the lighter the machine, the greater the effect made by the mass of the rider (and any passenger or luggage).

Because of the way in which the steering axis is inclined, turning the handlebar to the left moves the front tyre's contact patch to the right and vice versa. The front wheel also leans as well as turning, as shown in Fig. 15.

The bike is supported on an axis running between the two tyres (thin line Fig. 16). With the action of, say, turning the front wheel to the left, the centre of gravity remains to the left of the new axis shown by the broken line. In effect the centre of gravity is displaced to the left of the bike's new support axis. If there were no other forces acting on the machine it would now, under the force of gravity, topple over − towards the left.

If the bike were travelling along at low speed, centrifugal reaction to a left turn would make the bike want to fall over to the *right*; and the two forces would tend to cancel out. If they were not exactly equal the rider would have to compensate.

PRACTICAL STEERING

He could:

(a) increase the centrifugal force by going a little faster, or reduce it by going more slowly.

(b) change the centrifugal force by altering the steering; a tighter turn will increase the centrifugal force and it will also increase the distance by which the centre of gravity is displaced.

(c) move the centre of gravity by shifting his body weight.

In practice it will be a combination of all three and, in any given low speed manoeuvre, the rider will be making tiny alterations and corrections, balancing speed, steering and weight distribution against one another as he holds the bike on its course.

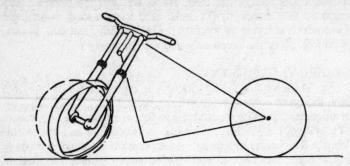

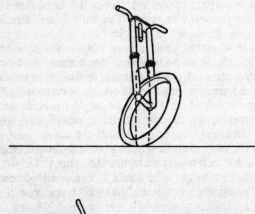

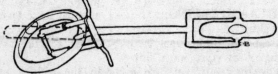

Fig. 15. When the front wheel is turned, the contact patch moves to the opposite side of the bike and the effects of castor make the wheel lean as well as displacing the contact area.

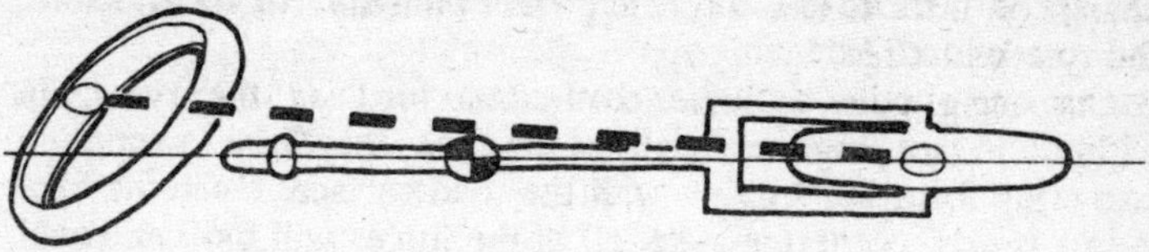

Fig. 16. Once you turn the front wheel, the centre of gravity — shown by black and white segmented circle — is no longer directly above the axis on which the bike is balancing (which is now the broken line instead of the thin one), so it tends to lean in the direction of the turn.

As speed rises above 15mph the steering method must shift — you will find you do it instinctively — to the technique for higher speeds already described. Instead of the necessary weight displacement (to counteract centrifugal force) occurring as a result of steering the way you want to go, at high speed it has to be made by leaning the machine over in that direction. As we have learned earlier the rider initiates the turn by pulling on the handlebar in the opposite direction in order to produce the lean required — *however, such a small force is needed that this is often done subconsciously* and many riders think that they corner only by leaning their bodies or by using knee pressure on the tank.

These two latter methods *will* steer the machine but the reactions they produce are extremely slow. For positive and rapid steering responses it is essential to use the handlebar. An obvious test of this statement is to try to steer without touching the handlebar — but do not move your hands too far away because you are about to find out that this statement is true ...

Depending on the individual machine's steering geometry and weight distribution, and even the types of tyres, it will need a force at the handlebar to persuade it to go from the vertical into a leaning position and it may need a continued force to hold it there. Alternatively, once there the "feel" of the steering may return to neutral.

HOW CORNERING FORCES BALANCE

In either case the bike will now be following a circular path. The cornering forces will be supplied by friction at the tyres and all the forces on the machine will balance out, as shown in Fig. 17. If they *don't* balance out, the bike will not be in a steady state;

it will not follow a regular, circular path; its leaning attitude will change or, if the load at a tyre is greater than the friction available, the tyre will slide.

Cornering puts a higher-than-usual load on the tyres. In addition to carrying the weight of the bike, they have to supply a cornering force via friction with the road surface. Once the bike is in a steady, cornering state, all of the forces will have an equal and opposite component and the resultant forces will act along the centre line of the bike, as in Fig. 17.

The horizontal cornering force combined with the bike's weight (always acting vertically) determines at what angle the bike must lean. When the cornering force equals the weight, the bike will lean at 45 degrees and the cornering force will be 1g. These additional forces resolve along the centre line of the bike and, as far as the suspension can tell, it's the same as carrying an extra load – therefore the springs compress a little further.

FEEDBACK

As a result of all this, the rider has the benefit of many sensations which can tell him how the machine is reacting and how close it is to the limits of roadholding.

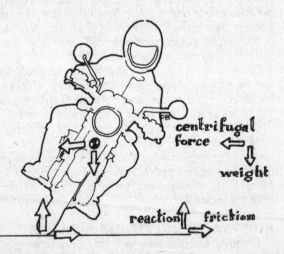

Fig. 17. Cornering forces balancing out in a leaning position.

First there is the force needed at the handlebar — which varies from machine to machine. Then there is the angle at which the machine is leaning, which the rider can only sense visually from his surroundings (as the forces all balance out, a glass of water on the fuel tank would have the surface of the liquid parallel to the rim of the glass, even when the motorcycle was banked at 45 degrees). Next the rider will sense his own apparent increase in weight as both gravity and centrifugal force act on his body. Cornering at 1g he will weigh 1.414 times his normal weight. For the mathematically minded this is explained as follows. The component at an angle to the line of a force is found by multiplying the force by the cosine of the angle. At 1g cornering the centrifugal force will equal the weight of the bike and rider, but will act horizontally. As the vertical and horizontal forces are equal, the bike will have to lean at 45 degrees. The components acting through the line of the motorcycle will then be weight × cos 45 and centrifugal force × cos 45. As these forces are equal, this is the same as weight × cos 45 × 2, or weight × 1.414.

An apparent increase in weight applies also to all of the bike and the extra load will make the suspension compress in proportion; the rider will feel this movement, and also notice the small changes which it produces in the steering geometry and the "feel" of the bike.

There is a final sensation which the rider may notice. This is sometimes called "drifting" and is caused by the bike travelling in a slightly different direction from that in which it is pointing. It is caused by slip at the tyres — without sliding or skidding they move a small amount sideways as well as travelling along in the normal sense. If both tyres do it together then in theory the bike moves to one side. If only the rear tyre slips (or slips more than the front tyre) which is the more usual and likely thing then the bike will actually turn into the bend. This movement is sometimes sufficient for the sensitive rider to detect.

The tyres only have a certain amount of grip and this is not influenced by direction. If the bike is travelling East-West and all the grip is used up by acceleration in this direction, then the slightest force towards the North will make the tyre move (slide) that way.

There are three conditions in which the machine can take a corner, as shown in Fig. 18. First in the centre drawing, with no tyre slip, both wheels follow a path about the same centre. The handlebars need to be turned towards the centre of the turn and it is likely that the rear wheel will follow a tighter radius and will

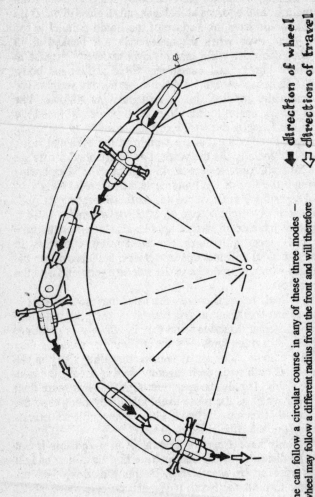

Fig. 18. A machine can follow a circular course in any of these three modes — note that the back wheel may follow a different radius from the front and will therefore have to rotate at a different speed. Also the tyre need not travel exactly in the direction in which it is pointing; the difference is called the slip angle and is actually much smaller than shown here.

therefore not need to travel as quickly as the front wheel.

There will be one set of conditions in which both wheels will travel along the same radius, at the same speed as depicted by the left hand drawing.

But the machine can still travel in a circular path without the handlebars being turned, as the third drawing shows. If the rear tyre is sufficiently loaded (by cornering force and by engine power) to generate slip, then the machine can travel along the course shown. Note that the rear wheel is following a larger radius and will therefore need to travel faster than the front wheel. Cornering under power or accelerating in a corner will tend to help this situation — and may also explain why machines often feel unsettled when the throttle is closed in a bend.

If the rear tyre had enough slip it would be necessary to turn the handlebars right in order for the machine to turn left.

Allowing the front tyre to slip would produce still more variations on this theme. Slip is not the same as slide — it can occur while the tyre still has rolling contact with the road and is not associated with any reduction in grip or loss of control. A sliding tyre by contrast will cause the same characteristics, only more so, and the sudden change in friction makes it very difficult to control.

RIDING POSITION

If you have practised making tight, low-speed turns, you will have noticed how the riding position is important; it not only makes control easier (or more difficult) it also helps steering and balance as the weight is shifted about.

The same applies to high-speed riding except that we now have two more considerations for riding comfort. One is against the mounting wind pressure, which begins to get noticeable above 45mph. The other is against road shocks which can still jolt the rider no matter how good the bike's suspension is. Fig. 19 shows a good riding position on both counts.

Here is shown how to use the riding position to swivel the rider forwards into a leaning stance. His body weight is naturally poised against wind pressure and is supported through the line of his legs as well as through the seat. He can quickly and easily, take weight through the footrests, avoiding the sudden jolt of road bumps and helping with general control.

The handlebars are at a height and width to give a natural, relaxed line to the arms. The body is in a good position to take the forces of acceleration, sharing the increased load fairly equally between seat, footrests and handlebar. Under braking the rider will have to move to a more upright position, straightening his arms to brace his body and possibly getting extra support by gripping the tank with his knees.

The benefits of a good position become much more noticeable in terms of comfort over long journeys, but they are still there for

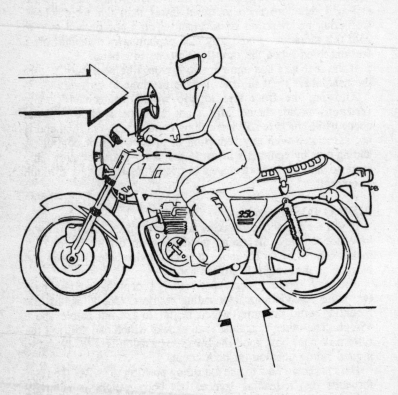

Fig. 19. Elements of a good riding position: the body is leaning forwards to balance wind pressure and can be supported through the legs and feet if the footrests are positioned well, helping control as well as absorbing road shocks. The arms are at a natural angle/height and can easily brace the rider under heavy braking.

short trips and they help to control the bike at all times.

In the sort of style to be avoided, wind pressure is allowed to push the rider back, and, as he has no support behind him or through his legs, his arms have to take the full strain. Every time the rear wheel hits a bump the jolt is fed straight into the rider's spine. The forces of acceleration and braking tend to make him slide up and down the seat with only his arms giving any support. Such a posture is poor and will cause all sorts of aches and pains after a journey of only an hour or so.

On many custom and even some factory built bikes, usually the ones having offbeat styling, a good riding position is almost impossible to attain. Indeed, most of them are very uncomfortable to ride for any length of time.

Riders in off-road competitions such as moto cross, trials and grass track racing know very well the advantages of being able to shift body weight quickly and easily. On slippery surfaces where slides can happen suddenly and unpredictably, it is essential to make use of every ounce of control and every millimetre of movement. They move forward and backwards to give each wheel maximum traction when they need to brake or accelerate; or if the acceleration would make the bike stand up on its back wheel, they shift forwards to reduce traction and hold the front down. And when they put the bike into a turn, they take weight on the outside foot, i.e. the right foot if the turn is to the left.

Then, if the bike slides it is an easy matter to shift the inside foot out for balance or support. The same thinking applies on a roadster; although slides are less likely, the heavier bikes are likely to wobble and need extra effort to make slow manoeuvres. In the same way, body position can help cornering control, by giving you the most freedom of movement and the most comfort.

BODY POSITION AND CORNERING CONTROL

Fig. 20 shows three basic variations: cornering with the body in-line with the bike; leaning further into the corner; and letting the bike lean while keeping the body closer to the vertical. It is not possible to say that any one of these is right or is better than others. Whatever feels best probably is best. In fact it is quite likely that each of the three styles will feel best suited to different conditions.

First, we deal with keeping the body upright and letting the bike lean. This can have advantages on poor surfaces or at low speeds when the bike is wriggled through a series of rapid manoeuvres like a slalom course. It allows the rider to take weight on the outer footrest, leaving the other foot free to be used for extra balance if need be. It gives the rider an emphasised feel to the bike's low angle of lean, making any changes that much more noticeable. For rapid manoeuvring it does not add the rider's momentum to the weight which has to be shifted from side to side, and this allows for faster responses.

At higher speeds most of these points are not necessary, being replaced by a need to exert a steady and precise input to the controls, and to receive as much feedback as possible. Many riders feel that it helps to move the body slightly ahead of the bike leaning themselves further into the turn. Possibly this amplifies the various sensations. One argument says that shifting the rider's weight into the turn means that the bike doesn't have to lean so far, and is therefore less likely to slide. This is undeniable, although the degree to which it happens is debatable, particularly with a heavy bike and a light rider. Possibly it just feels more comfortable — which is justification enough.

If neither of these styles offers any advantage (real or imaginary) then you may as well stay where you are, in-line with the bike, which is the third alternative.

Normally you would expect to have maximum control with both feet on the footrests. Even on slippery surfaces such as hard-packed snow, you will only lose balance by trying to paddle along with both feet on the ground. Despite this there are obviously times when you have to put out a foot to avoid falling down altogether and these occasions can be divided into two groups. First to support or correct a sliding bike. Second to regain balance while riding very slowly.

If the bike is sliding because it has suddenly gone on to a very slippery surface, such as ice, and you don't really expect to regain control then obviously you need to get your leg out from under the bike before it falls over. With one leg out, speedway style, you may find that the steering still has some effect and you may be able to ride the slide out. At least if the bike goes all the way over onto its side you'll be able to get off on the low side and keep the bike in front of you.

If the bike slides on an otherwise reasonable surface it can be corrected by *easing* off the power and lifting the bike slightly (that is, returning towards upright from being banked over). Shutting the throttle quickly — or doing anything too suddenly — can either make the slide worse, or give the tyres such sudden grip that they flip the bike upright and throw the rider over the top.

The slide may not happen slowly enough or predictably enough

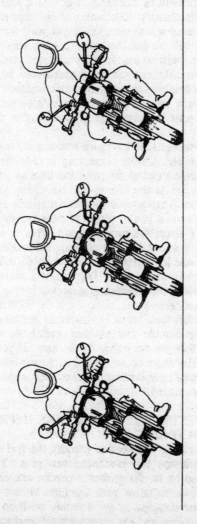

Fig. 20. Shifting the body can help to manoeuvre the bike, as explained in the text. Keeping the body upright can help slow speed control, especially on slippery surfaces, while leaning into the turn may be easier at higher speeds.

to be corrected on the throttle and it will then be necessary to use a foot. The important thing is to put your foot in the right place and to do it quickly, because as soon as the ground hits your boot, it will grip it and try to pull you backwards off the bike. So it needs to be a swift, firm kick, strong enough to lift the bike and regain full tyre grip and fast enough not to cause you to lose control again.

When either wheel slides outwards, the bike's angle of lean increases (until it eventually falls over). This happens all too quickly and by the time you've decided to put your foot down to steady the bike, it will be leaning quite a long way. To put it another way, the floor will no longer be in the same place, relative to your foot. You should not put your foot *down* but move it *outwards*, ideally holding it momentarily until the floor comes up and meets it. This way you get more leverage from your leg and you will not push your foot into the ground harder than you'd expected to.

Putting a foot to the ground to regain low-speed balance is an entirely different matter. Unlike correcting a slide, you should take your time, reaching out as far from the bike as you can, to get maximum leverage. As the bike is still travelling, you should stretch forwards, too, putting your foot down firmly and letting the bike ride past it, so that you've plenty of time to regain balance before lifting your foot off the ground again. This is a lot more effective than sticking a foot down at random and making a series of short hops, each one inducing a counter-wobble until you have to put the other foot down as well. The use of a foot in a slide situation and for low speed balance is depicted by Fig. 21.

In your early practice sessions, away from the road, it's worth trying really tight, full lock turns as slowly as the bike will go. Take weight on the outside footrest and stretch forwards and outwards with the foot on the inside of the turn. If you can put your toes down in the exact centre of the turn, you can ride the bike all the way round, pirouetting on your toes without sliding your foot along the ground.

PERSONAL ADJUSTMENTS WHICH MAY IMPROVE YOUR BIKE'S HANDLING

For normal road riding you need to identify the feel of various controls and to cultivate the feedback they give. The bike's response is governed by its design but it can be altered slightly, as follows. If you plan to tailor your machine to suit your own preferences, the first thing is to get a riding position which is comfortable. Other items and the changes they produce are:

component	change	effect
handlebar	wider	makes steering lighter
wheelbase	longer	makes steering slower, increases bike's stability
	shorter	faster steering response, less high-speed stability
castor	steeper	faster steering, lighter feel, more likely to wobble at high speed
	shallower	slower steering, heavier feel
trail	more	heavier steering
	less	lighter steering

The castor and trail can be altered by raising or lowering the front and rear suspension — an adjustment provided on some machines, or effected by using different damper units. Raising the back of the bike or lowering the front will make the castor angle steeper.

Finally tyres can make the biggest differences of all. You should stick to the recommended sizes and pressures but different makes of tyre can give completely different handling, characteristics. Unfortunately each combination of bike and tyre can only be evaluated by trial and error; there are no generalisations which are always true for all machines.

PILLION PASSENGERS

Whilst on the subject of handling note that pillion passengers can have a large effect on the way a bike responds, especially if they move about. You should make sure that they understand that they are not to lean in or out when the bike is cornering. It helps if they have a grab rail to hold on to and if you do not destroy their confidence by sudden acceleration or hard braking. Learner riders are not allowed to carry passengers.

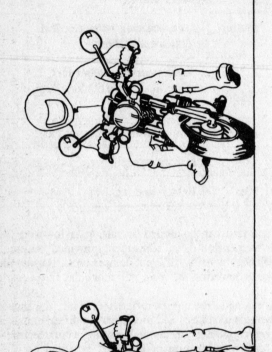

Fig. 21. To use a foot for low-speed balance, reach forwards and away from the bike as in the left-hand picture to get the maximum effect. To correct a slide, move the foot out rather than down and let the floor come up to meet it.

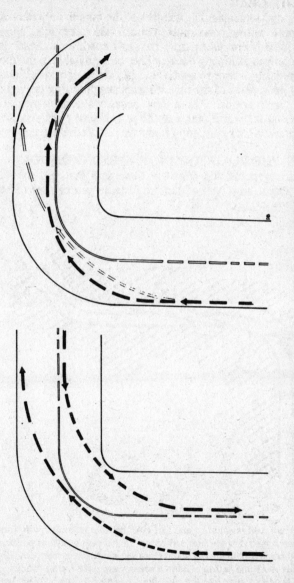

Fig. 22. On the open road the best line to take is the one which gives the best visibility through the bend — shown (left) for left- and right-handed corners. Decelerate or brake on the approach and accelerate evenly all the way through the corner. On blind bends (right) hold a wider than normal approach (solid line) which allows you more time for extra braking and makes it easier to adjust your line if the bend should tighten up or be obstructed.

THE RIGHT GEAR

Knowing and understanding the feel of the bike is only part of the problem; having maximum control also depends upon (accurate) information taken from the road conditions ahead. It depends upon you following the best line, on being able to put the machine precisely where you want it to be, at the right speed and in the right gear. Most of the time it's easy and choosing the right gear, etc., isn't critical. On a few occasions it becomes so imperative that it's worth planning the rest of your riding on the assumption that a tricky situation is always just around the corner.

READING THE ROAD FOR HIGH SPEED CONTROL

As a starting point, the *Highway Code* says that you should always be able to stop well within the distance you can see to be

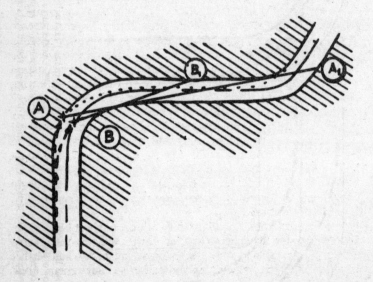

Fig. 23. Correct road positioning and line give the rider maximum visibility and let approaching traffic see him earlier too. In this case a rider at position A has held position over to the left until he can see where the corner goes. His line of sight is A-A1 and he can pick up a smooth approach for the following left-hander. If he had gone into the right-hander earlier (position B) his line of sight would only be B-B1 and his riding line would take him out to the left after the right-hander, making a poor approach to the left-hander.

clear. This is the only defensible advice which can be given but there are obviously occasions, such as overtaking, when the philosophy is stretched pretty thinly. It is essential to recognise when you are at a greater than usual risk and to have an idea of how much more risk there is.

For example, the faster you go, the further ahead you need to plan. If you double your speed there are a lot of good reasons for suggesting that you quadruple your viewing distance. You don't have to be going very quickly before you need to be taking in quite a vast area ahead and to the sides.

In this area, a lot can be happening. There will be bits which are temporarily hidden or disguised as a bending road unwinds, and small hills and dips obscure the road surface. You can increase your visibility and keep more options open by choosing the best line to follow.

A classical line through curves is shown in the left hand diagram of Fig. 22. On a left-hand bend, start near the centre of the road, slowing all the way to the bend until you can see where it is going. Then you can sweep through on the widest possible radius. A right hander would similarly be approached from the left side of the road, these wide approaches giving maximum visibility through the corner (see Fig. 23) and allowing approaching traffic to get the earliest glimpse of yourself. Where the curve looks as if it is followed by several others, or as if it may double back on itself as in the right-hand part of Fig. 22 you will need to get the earliest warning and maximise your room to manoeuvre. As explained in the caption, approach it in a straight line so that any additional braking can be done, as always, well before you get into the corner itself and you will be going slowly enough to choose your optimum line once you see how the road is going to open up.

Roads have vertical "bends" too and these, or short hedgerows, are often enough to conceal a low car. Larger vehicles on the same stretch of road can add to the deception as you tend to believe that if you can see one vehicle you are able to see any others. Look at Fig. 24.

Remember, this sort of road positioning is for relatively high speed riding on open country roads; it is *not* always compatible with other traffic behaviour and it is for you to make necessary allowances. For example, you may have to hold the bike to one side of your lane before making a left or right turn at a junction. Also, if you are going to move from one side of a lane to the other, it is imperative to take account of traffic coming up behind.

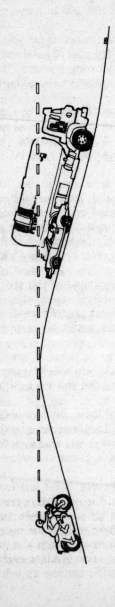

Fig. 24. Roads have vertical "bends". The rider's sight-line here spotlights one danger.

7
Traffic

So far the motorcycle has been considered pretty much on its own when, in fact, the biggest problems come from other traffic. The rules, regulations and conventions for road use are all set out clearly in the *Highway Code* and there isn't much to be gained by simply repeating them all here — except to say that the onus is on the individual to know and understand traffic laws.

POSITIONING

To deal with other traffic it is important to stick to two basic principles. One is to keep a close watch on your immediate surroundings. The second is to position yourself so that everyone else can figure out where you are planning to go.

Even that does not cover all eventualities. The police teach what they call "defensive driving", which isn't a bad idea. Ultimately, if you regarded all other traffic as belligerent and deliberately trying to run into you, you would position yourself so that they couldn't collide with you even if they wanted to. That simply is not possible all of the time but going a little less quickly, leaving slightly bigger gaps and seeing how much you can learn from other people's antics is good riding.

Your own road positioning is important, even if there appears to be no other traffic on your particular stretch of road. Cars often swing out of driveways or side roads into the path of a motorcyclist; it is in your interest to make yourself as prominently visible as possible, not close to the kerb or to parked cars, and to leave yourself a possible escape route as you approach junctions with side roads.

LOOKING BEHIND

As you ride along, either keep a running check in the mirrors or turn your head to look behind. It is essential and a test requirement to look over your shoulder before you move off from the kerb, overtake, pull in to stop, or turn to one side, but you should not only look at these times, you should know what is going on behind you all of the time.

SIGNALLING

Signal your *intentions,* always. A signal given at the instant you change course is *too late.* Those around you need to know what you are going to do next more than what you are doing now, although usually it will make sense to continue a flashing signal during a complete manoeuvre.

On test you may be asked to give arm signals in addition to flashing ones for part of the test route or, you may be asked questions about them separately. The examiner will want to be sure you understand and can give the arm signals correctly as well as satisfying himself as to your competence in using your flashing indicators. If during your test an occasion arises where an arm signal would be helpful or might add safety, then − just as you would in normal riding − give it.

RIGHT AND LEFT TURNS

When you plan to turn off a main road at a junction, it is important that the sequence of events is begun early enough. Look behind, signal if necessary and get into position on the road, e.g. over to the left if you plan to turn left, adjust your speed, change down through the gears so you are prepared to move on after the corner, look behind again, signal, make the turn, cancel the signal and make a fresh check on your new surroundings.

Problems occur if there are several turnings or if the turning is obscured by a parked car, etc. You should normally signal as early as possible, but here you may need to make it obvious which turning you plan to take. The risk is that a driver waiting to pull out of another opening shortly before your turning may assume that you plan to turn off earlier (into his road) and may drive out in front of you. Do not begin to signal left until it must be obvious to such a driver that you do not mean to turn down his road. There is a similar danger if ever you forget to cancel the indicator switch and ride along oblivious to the fact your indicator is winking away. Note that other drivers and riders can make the same mistake ...

Where the turning is obscured, the only solution is to slow down much more than would be normal and not to make any assumptions at all about what anyone else is going to do or that you may be going to find the junction empty when you arrive.

Right turns off a main road are more risky because you have to turn across the traffic stream. You need to take up position near the centre of the road well in advance and signal clearly. Get down the gears ready to make the turn in one but if you have to stop in the centre of the road while oncoming traffic goes past, pull up in a straight line and do not wobble to either side.

If you have to stop and wait, keep the machine facing straight ahead and don't turn the front wheel towards the right. The reason for this is that you are at risk of being shunted from behind and while this is bad enough, if the bike or the steering is pointed to the right, you will be pushed in this direction, into the oncoming traffic. Keep one brake on, so that the indicator is augmented by the bright tail light to make you as conspicuous as possible.

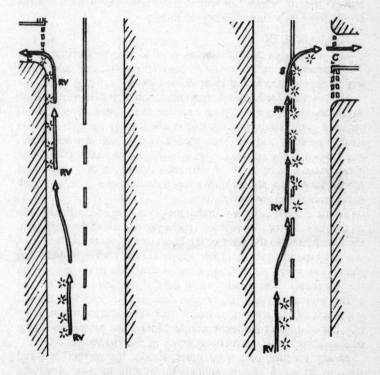

Fig. 25. The sequence for any change of position/direction, shown here as simple left and right turns. Check behind (RV = rear vision), signal and move into the appropriate lane or road position. Hold that line and signal for the turn (shown by the flashes); emphasise with arm signals if necessary. If turning across the traffic flow, be prepared to stop (at the point S in the diagram). Check behind before making the turn in a steady, smooth sweep, to bring you into a good position on the new road, as shown by C, but this might vary depending on visibility into the junction, parked cars on the new road, etc.

As well as the oncoming traffic to your right there will be traffic behind you which will try to pass on your left. Make sure nobody is trying to overtake on your *right* last thing before you make the turn. Fig. 25 shows the proper sequence for such events.

Note that footpaths are deemed to cross road junctions and this often gives pedestrians the right of way, especially where minor roads emerge onto a main road. It always pays to make allowances for pedestrians, particularly if they show no sign of being aware of your presence − they may step out suddenly into the road. Irrespective of "rights" of way it is far better to be aware of the possibility and to leave plenty of room.

ROUNDABOUTS

The whole idea of roundabouts is to do away with right turns. They direct the entire traffic stream into a circular orbit from which people turn left at their chosen exits.

This is fine, although it may mean changing lane − which would also be fine if everyone travelled at the same speed and left sensible gaps. Unfortunately this is not usually the case, so you have to position yourself with great care to make sure you arrive at your exit in the left lane. One advantage of a motorcycle is that it can make a right, a left or a centre channel out of a single lane road. Many roundabouts now have more than one lane, in which case choose the appropriate one.

Traffic approaching a roundabout gives way to traffic already on the roundabout. If you intend taking an exit off to the right, join the roundabout to the right of the lane (or the righthand lane). As you go around, getting closer to your exit, traffic to your left should disappear at previous exits, leaving you room to move to the left (lane). You should watch out for traffic to your left and adjust your speed and position so that you *can* move to the left without clashing with other traffic and in good time to make the exit. Signalling at roundabouts should follow the principles shown in Fig. 26 and the instructions given in the *Highway Code*.

At any junction plan your route, choose the correct lane and stick to it, going slowly enough to be able to take in all the information from road signs. Even if you make a mistake carry on until you are clear of the junction. Or, on a roundabout go round for a full circuit.

FOLLOWING TOO CLOSELY

Most of a motorcylist's problems stem from his bike being smaller and more manoeuvrable than other vehicles, a fact often unrecognised by other drivers.

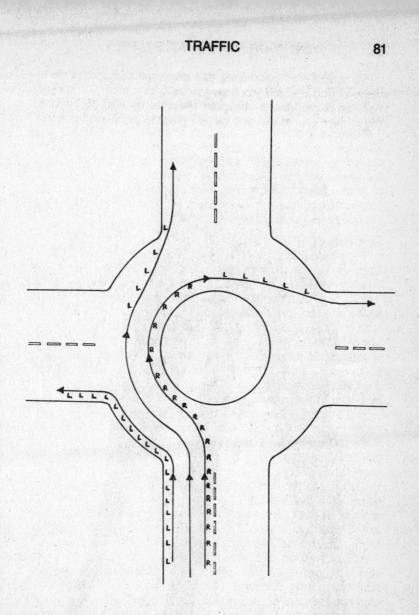

Fig. 26. The idea of roundabouts is to avoid right turns, instead routing everyone so that they turn left at their exit. Choose your approach position (or lane) accordingly, allowing room for other traffic. This shows the right way to use your indicators on a roundabout, represented by the letters L and R.

This makes road positioning that much more important. In a stream of traffic which you hope gradually to overtake, it is easy to get too close. Make a conscious effort to stay well back and a little to the right, so that you can see past the car ahead but keep

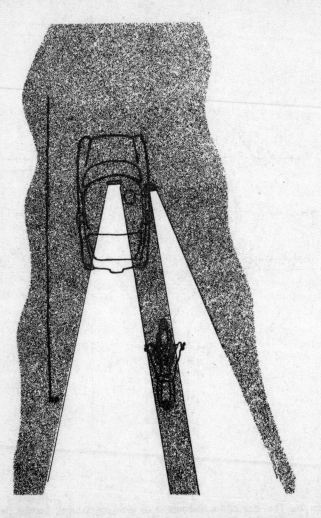

Fig. 27. Following too closely to other traffic, or in the vehicle's "blind" spot can leave a motorcyclist in great danger from sudden stops or turns made by its driver.

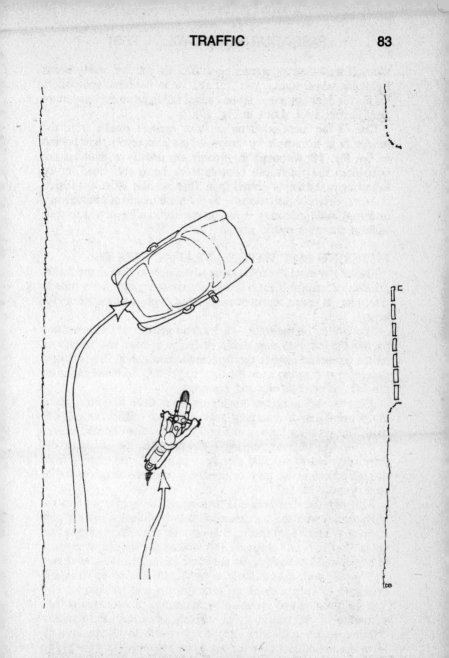

Fig. 28. One of the classic car/bike incidents is the right turn without warning, as a bike is overtaking or following.

yourself well clear of oncoming traffic! (If you are nearly in his right-side wheel tracks, you will also be in the blind spot where his mirror does not see — if you cannot safely move over any more *drop further back*. Look at Fig. 27).

One of the most common car/bike crashes results from the sudden right-turn made by the car with a motorcycle right behind it. See Fig. 28. Although the drivers are usually at fault for not signalling, the riders can contribute by being too close, or by following in the driver's blind spot. This can also cause a collision if the car driver simply stops — as people often do at roundabouts or complicated junctions — just as you are looking across to your right at the other traffic stream.

FILTERING PAST WAITING TRAFFIC QUEUES

One of the motorcycle's biggest advantages is that as the traffic grinds to a standstill there is usually room enough for a bike to filter past. It seems innocent enough but there can be a lot of risk here.

Try to filter on the right — drivers do not expect bikes to come past on the left; they may suddenly decide to drive two wheels up on the pavement outside the first newsagent's shop they see or a passenger may swing open the door to get out. So if the gap is on the left, go extra slowly and carefully.

It is also easy to go too quickly on the right — forgetting about the possibilities of emerging pedestrians or traffic from a side road. One problem here is, as Fig. 29 shows, that once the stream of traffic has stopped, leaving a gap for him, the emerging car driver may not be worried about any more vehicles coming from that direction — he may be too busy concentrating on traffic coming from his left.

Although the slim lines of a motorcycle can help it get through traffic jams with the minimum of delay, while it is going past stationary, snarled-up traffic, it is easy for the rider to forget that not *all* traffic is at a standstill. As well as the sudden emergence of cars from side roads, there are other motorcycles; so, as shown by Fig. 32, even if both lanes of traffic are choked up, it is still necessary to keep a check on your mirrors and all around.

If the queue of cars is caused by an unusual problem rather than a routine set of traffic lights, drivers often decide to take a different route, and swing out of the stream to U-turn around. Most drivers, unless they happen to be motorcyclists as well, do not even think of the possibility of a bike coming up from behind — all traffic has reached a stop as far as they are concerned.

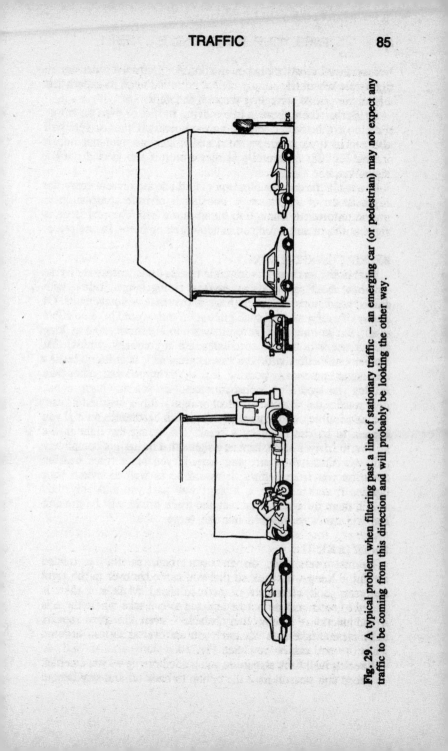

Fig. 29. A typical problem when filtering past a line of stationary traffic — an emerging car (or pedestrian) may not expect any traffic to be coming from this direction and will probably be looking the other way.

Unless they have handled a motorcycle themselves drivers in tightly packed traffic simply cannot be relied upon to expect that a bike may come wriggling through the gaps.

Similarly, where there is free-moving traffic, or even an empty road, do not be fooled into going too quickly. Other drivers will also regard it as an empty road and might just pull out into it without looking as carefully as they would if you were driving a 32-ton truck.

In most of these examples you may think the drivers carry the largest share of the blame — but that is of little consolation to anyone unfortunate enough to bump into them. The real issue is not about right and wrong; it is about getting home in one piece.

BEING CONSPICUOUS

To this end, various motorcycling bodies have expressed diverse opinions about such aids as daytime riding lamps, riding with dipped headlamps, bright clothing, and even day-glo oversuits. Of course, if everyone used such gimmicks, they would have no effect at all. But as long as motorcyclists are in a minority and as long as the users of visual stimulants are a minority within that minority, the effect will be about as great as it is going to be. As it also costs practically nothing, it could be argued that, other than making you look a bit foolish, it cannot do you any harm. And, if it prevents the slightest accident or injury, it has justified its use.

One possible disadvantage of riding with headlamps on is if you happen to be overtaken by a truck. On seeing the light in his mirror, the driver may take it as a signal that he has got completely past you, and swing into your lane. If you see a truck bearing down on you from behind, it would be as well to switch your lights off, wait until he is a short way past you and only then switch them on again. That way the truck driver will be grateful and you won't get mashed into the verge.

OVERTAKING

Normal overtaking, on an open road, should be treated carefully. Keep well back so that you can edge over to the right and get a good, clear view of the road ahead. Make sure there is plenty of room and do not be tempted to overtake where there is a road junction — or any other obstacle — even if the road appears to be clear. Make sure whatever you are overtaking can have no reason to pull out on you. See Fig. 30.

Keeping well back also gives you a good run up — you can pick up speed and yet still have the option to back off and stay behind the vehicle in front. Take a good look behind to make sure that no-one is about to overtake *you* — use the right indicator and go! Aim to get past as quickly and decisively as possible — you are at extra risk when you are on the wrong side of the road. Remember to cancel your indicator when you are past.

One problem with lightweight machines is that they can easily pick up speed in the slipstream of a larger vehicle such as a truck. This lets them pull out and get rapidly past ... until they reach a point close to the front of the other vehicle where they come out of the slipstream and feel the full force of wind resistance. Often it slows the bike so much that it cannot complete the overtaking manoeuvre and this is quite an alarming discovery to make.

It is important — on low-powered machines — not to rely on the slipstream of leading vehicles; do not be tempted to overtake unless you know you can get past. At lower speeds change down through the gears to get more acceleration to pass things quickly.

Fig. 31 shows some more matters to ponder in respect of overtaking.

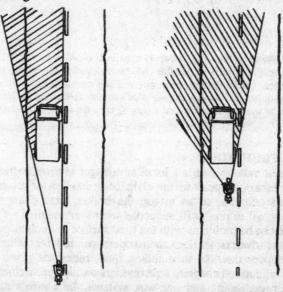

Fig. 30. Overtaking view. Getting too close obscures the field of view, as in the right-hand example. Just by dropping back and careful positioning, as in the left-hand drawing, the rider can see more, other traffic (including the overtakee) can see him, there is room to get a run-up and pick up enough speed to complete the manoeuvre in the minimum of time.

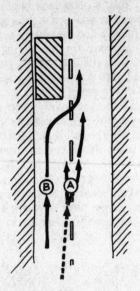

Fig. 31. Overtaking line. This can apply to parked objects or moving vehicles. Get into position as early as possible (A), having checked thoroughly behind and signalled. Unlike the rider at B who will pop out suddenly from behind the vehicle/object, a rider at A can see what's coming (and it can see him) and will get more warning of pedestrians emerging from the far side of a stationary vehicle.

TOWN TECHNIQUE

Riding a motorcycle has a lot of advantages in town traffic, but it is necessary to practise the right co-ordination of all of the machine's controls, so as to use the brakes, gear change and indicators, all in one swift sequence whenever required.

There can be problems with the road surface — such as poorly repaired roadworks, steel manhole covers, painted lines which are more slippery than the surrounding road, raised cat's-eyes and, worst of all, raised concrete lane dividers on the approach/exit to various roundabouts and one-way systems. In fast-moving but closely-packed traffic it can be very difficult to spot these hazards in time to avoid them without any potentially dangerous swerves.

On unfamiliar roads it is all very well remembering the possibilities of such hazards — it is often another matter to do something about it. If you drop well back from the vehicle ahead, another will squeeze into the space. If you go slowly enough to give yourself a fair chance, you will end up being forced into the gutter, where it is likely that you will find even more debris. There is no single answer when you are in the middle of a traffic stream, except to maintain as much room as you can around you and to remember the risks of running over obstacles in the road.

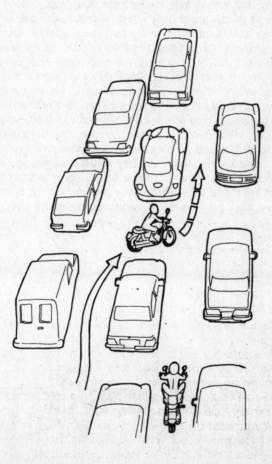

Fig. 32. Filtering through dense traffic is not without problems from people opening car doors or making sudden turns. There may also be other motorcyclists coming up behind, or changing lane, as well.

A similar problem arises on wet city roads, which can be made very slippery by rubber and oil deposits. Car drivers often do not appreciate the surface changes, or if they do they take no notice. What could be a minor slide in a car might have serious consequences for a motorcycle.

Again, the rider is often faced with the prospect of keeping up with the traffic at a speed which may be too fast for safety, or easing up and having cars try to force their way past.

These problems are at their worst on fast, multi-lane city roads during the rush-hour when everyone's main interest seems to be to keep going at the greatest possible rate before the real traffic jams begin. There is another ever-present danger for the motorcyclist — that of being squashed — as shown by Fig. 33. Work out where other vehicles are likely to go, stay away from gaps that are likely to close up and position your bike so that other drivers can see where you want to go and can leave you room.

This is often made difficult by the legal restriction of inexperienced riders to small and low-powered machines. A moped, for example, would be very difficult to manage on many parts of London's North Circular road. There are even places where it would be difficult to cross such a road on a moped. If a machine does not have the performance to keep up with the flow

Fig. 33. Thoughtless road positioning can cause problems as well, as shown here. The back wheels of long vehicles do not follow the track of the front wheels, but "cut" the corner.

of traffic, it is extremely difficult to filter to the right-hand lane in order to get into position for a right turn.

The rider can signal his hopeful intention and rely upon a following driver making room for him. Since this cannot be guaranteed it is not unknown for a rider to abandon making a right turn, and to go past the junction and make three left turns around the next block instead.

One further problem, which the rider may not be aware of until it is too late, is caused by the exotic styling of many of the low-powered machines. Restricted, like mopeds, to a particular power output, the manufacturers have to rely upon this means to attract customers and so the machines intentionally look like much bigger and more powerful devices. Who can blame a disinterested car driver for assuming that such a machine will move as quickly as other motorcycles he has encountered? There is quite a real risk of being rammed from behind or even from the side by drivers who seriously expect more performance, based on looks.

It is hard to see what the rider can do to avoid this sort of problem — other than wobbling, looking a bit insecure and hoping that the message will carry across the street, although these are the things that he has been trying expressly not to do ever since he got his machine.

Maybe the reasoning is that if a novice can come to terms with such a bike in bad traffic conditions, then he will surely be able to handle anything.

8
In the City

In theory the same rules and conventions apply whether you're riding along a deserted road, in a small country town or in the middle of the city rush hour. However, city conditions occasionally get so overcrowded that it is necessary to streamline things just to keep everyone moving. In traffic which is either moving very slowly or not at all, it is often permissible to take liberties which would be too risky if the traffic stream were moving at a higher speed.

CUSTOM AND COMMONSENSE

Filtering from a minor road into a stream of traffic is a typical example; if drivers in the main stream leave a reasonable gap other drivers can join the steam without causing anyone any difficulties or delays. Motorcycles can take advantage of slightly smaller gaps but remember, the motorcyclist is more vulnerable. In this sort of situation make sure that there *is* enough of a gap and that the approaching driver is aware of what you are about to do. If you suspect he may not have seen you or if he could be going to accelerate, wait for the next opportunity.

In everyday riding there are dozens of situations like this. As the traffic speeds back up to its normal rate then riders and drivers must switch back to the more formal highway manners − and it is during this interim period, or when someone is in a particular hurry, that there is most likely to be a misunderstanding. Car drivers have the advantage of being surrounded by a fairly well designed box − built expressly to absorb the sort of impact which could so easily follow from any "misunderstanding". Motorcyclists are at a distinct disadvantage and one which they would do well not to forget.

Roads used by heavy traffic usually have their lanes marked by the dark stains of tyres, fuel and oil. These deposits can be slippery, especially after rain, and should be avoided as much as possible.

When you have to stop, at traffic lights for example, pull over to one side of the lane. This will leave room for anyone following who may have misjudged the junction and it will take you off the well-used bit of road on to a grippier surface which will help with your final braking and when you come to accelerate away.

It is easy enough to anticipate the changing of traffic signals by watching the lights controlling the crossroad but resist the temptation to whizz away as soon as you get a green light. There is always the late arrival who thinks he can squeeze across the junction as his lights switch to red; and on the opposite side of your road there is often someone waiting to turn right who figures that if he anticipates the lights he can zoom across before your column of traffic gets moving.

SLIPPERY SURFACES

As well as the normal deposits left by traffic, there are other very slippery surfaces which crop up regularly. The worst, by far, is spilt gas oil or diesel which is reasonably invisible and, unlike petrol, does not evaporate particularly quickly. This often swills out of the tanks of trucks and buses as they swing around roundabouts and junctions — the worst places are any sharp corners near a large depot, bus station or garage. Usually the first warning you get is the unmistakable smell which, depending on which way the wind is blowing, gives you a short space of time before your wheels start sliding. The best thing to do is straighten the bike up, slow down and keep it as upright as possible until you're clear of the danger. Remember though that if you're following the culprit, there's likely to be a trail of oil around the next corner, too!

Steel manhole covers, steel studs used to mark out crossings and cat's-eyes are all slippery when they are wet and will make tyres slide as they go across them, if the bike is at all banked over. However, unless the machine is really being cornered hard, the tyres will grip once more when they again meet the road surface. There shouldn't be too much of a problem but they are unsettling and it's better to avoid the things altogether.

What is even more slippery, yet often looks quite innocent, is the finishing surface put onto road repairs. Where the new surface meets the old there is often a seam of black shiny stuff which makes a neat repair but is a lot more slippery than the surrounding tarmac. It is worse when the line of repairs runs parallel with the road and there is a chance that the machine will run along the slippery seam. The danger signs are that the bike will start to twitch from side to side — ultimately one wheel will break away and turn completely to one side. To keep control, ease off the power but don't shut the throttle completely and gently veer away from the slippery line.

All oil-based surfaces are likely to be slippery when they are new.

On any slippery surface make all movements as smoothly and as gently as possible — you should aim to do this all the time because it's not something you'll learn the first time you get caught in a shower.

PREDICTING TRAFFIC FLOW

As the lines of traffic come to a standstill, you'll find yourself filtering past the queues. Keep as far away as you can (depending on oncoming traffic, etc.) watching out for danger areas ahead — such as tall vehicles, suspicious gaps in the line of cars, a glimpse of pedestrians about to cross between the stationary cars, the flashing of headlamps up ahead.

When the traffic is crawling along you will inevitably be riding very closely to other vehicles. As the stream starts to move faster again, it is an easy mistake to maintain this distance instead of letting the gap open up as you all go quicker. You'll need larger gaps not only because you need more room to stop but also because your field of view is more restricted when you're up close to another vehicle.

It's important to keep sight of what's going on some little way ahead. When you see the brake lights coming on, you must be prepared to stop or slow down yourself, even if you haven't been able to see what caused the hold-up.

At the same time you'll notice regular traffic patterns developing, typically as drivers wait to turn right and other vehicles may or may not be able to squeeze past (see Fig. 34); or as buses and trucks skew across the road and block two lanes. As you come to recognize these recurring manoeuvres you'll find gaps opening up which a motorcycle can make use of while larger vehicles are standing waiting.

As you see a pattern developing you can get your machine into position to take advantage of it, or alternatively to avoid the problems it may cause. By taking things easily, holding back, and watching you'll see how the problems are caused and you'll probably find that your own journey is made a little easier and faster because of it.

When it comes to traffic problems, motorcyclists have the advantage that they can get past a jam and can see the way the traffic has built up, the factors that led up to it and how much room has been used up in the process. Car drivers usually only see the back of the car in front.

To take one example, where there are two lanes of traffic going in the same direction. A car in the right-hand lane gets to a

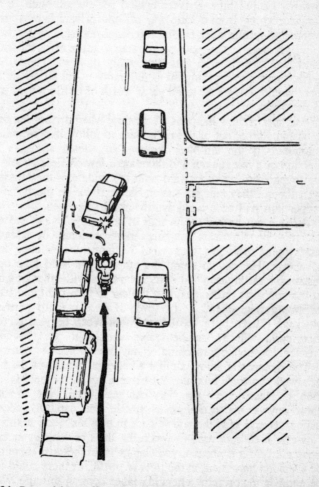

Fig. 34. Recognising traffic patterns can help smooth, safe progress. Cars waiting to turn often stop the traffic behind, although a motorcycle can get up to the front of the queue. Then you either wait for the car to turn off (which will leave you with a clear path) or you may be able to make use of the solo bike's lack of width quite safely to get through the gap, as long as you know that the driver on the left has seen what you are doing.

junction and wants to turn right but cannot because there is a lot of traffic coming from the opposite direction. Because he does not pull over far enough, the vehicle on his left cannot get past: such a vehicle is shown waiting in the left lane in Fig. 34 with a queue growing behind him. Drivers behind see the car with its right indicator going from a long way off and drivers have a morbid aversion to getting stuck behind someone waiting to turn right. So, some way back up the road, people start to make dives for the left-hand lane, which soon gets thoroughly blocked. The tail-back quickly grows to anything up to 100 yards — but all in one lane; there would only be 50 to 60 yards worth of traffic if they stayed in two lanes.

This sort of thing happens all the time when drivers see people up ahead getting out of the right lane; to follow suit seems to be automatic. If the tail-back happens to stretch across a busy junction or a roundabout and there are a few clueless people who are prepared to move forward onto the middle of the crossroads even though they can see the traffic is stuck on the far side, a proper jam will be created swiftly in all directions.

Perhaps not having the benefit of seeing the cause and effect prevents people from making more rational decisions. A motorcyclist who has seen what is happening is at a double advantage. He can go along the empty right-hand lane on the reasonable assumption that fairly soon there will either be a break in the opposing traffic enabling the car to turn right and leaving an empty road ahead — or (even if it is a more permanent blockage caused by a breakdown) that when he gets there the motorcycle will be manoeuvrable enough to get around the problem, without encroaching on any other vehicle's road space.

The motorcycle enjoys similar advantages whenever the traffic gets well and truly blocked. By being a couple of feet higher up than most car drivers, the rider can get a better view of what is ahead anyway and can approach traffic jams carefully, choosing the best course with the widest gaps to take his machine through. However there is a need to watch the lines of vehicles carefully, particularly if it is necessary to change lanes, because there might be a sudden movement in the flow of traffic, or there could easily be another motorcyclist changing lanes coming through another gap (see Fig. 32).

In traffic jams where there are long queues, drivers often stagger their positions out to one side in an attempt to see beyond the vehicle in front. A gap between two lanes can therefore diminish and frequently such a space can no longer be called a gap.

This makes it tempting for a rider to zig-zag through the first suitable opening he sees, into the next lane, which could be a bit embarrassing if there happens to be another motorcycle hurtling along that lane. One moral is to take a lot of care if you intend to zig-zag; the other moral is not to hurtle between lanes of traffic. There are also strict rules about changing lanes in the *Highway Code* with which riders must comply.

WHICH SIDE TO OVERTAKE?

Overtaking is an area where our risks are heavily increased not only through any oncoming traffic, but because it brings us so close tc whatever we are passing. The convention is that we overtake on the right. The slower driver will naturally expect faster things to go past on his right. An offshoot of this is that he does not so readily expect things to pass on his left, even in a one-way street where you might think he ought to; he is more likely to turn left without looking or signalling than he is to turn right.

So if you filter between stopped lines of traffic, or sneak through on the left of a trickling queue *be aware* of the possibilities of people moving into your road space.

The *Highway Code* lists a few exceptions to the "pass on the right" convention, when you may pass on the left; amongst them are:

1. When queues of traffic side by side are moving slowly — this, as suggested, is fairly safe — provided any movement is obvious and there is nowhere for anyone to make a sudden left turn cutting across from outside you. You are expressly forbidden to chop and change lanes in order to gain advantage.

2. In one-way systems (but note that a dual carriageway is *not* a one-way street).

3. When the driver in front intends to turn right — again this should be safe, as long as you are certain that he *is* going to turn right, as long as he does not obscure your view of the way ahead and you will not cut in front of other drivers.

4. Where your intention is to turn left shortly or park; you must in this case also move to the left lane to do so if you are not already in it.

Whenever stream speed has built up, and everyone is bowling along, be it single lane, dual carriageway, or motorway, you *only* overtake on the right (unless a *Highway Code* exception applies). Some motorcyclists seem to imagine they are excluded from the rules, perhaps because they can slip between lanes of bunching traffic while it thunders along — but just because they can do it does *not* give them the right to do it. There are always the risks of someone changing lane, of a vehicle emerging from a side road and so on. To let an insurance company or a magistrates court have to confirm this is a pretty dumb approach.

All this has a corollary too. Other people will prefer to overtake you on your right. Do not deny them this. Move to the lane which is furthest to the left; keep as left as possible except when you are overtaking; leave the right lanes vacant. It works in your favour, ultimately, because when someone does come to overtake you, he will be encouraged to pass on your right and at least you know which side to expect faster traffic to appear. This particularly applies to multi-lane roads such as dual carriageways and motorways where there is usually a wide mixture of fast and slow traffic. With all lanes moving along well there is no excuse for obstructing an outer lane, but neither is someone else doing so to be regarded as an excuse to pass that person on the inside.

PROCEDURE FOR RIGHT TURNS AT CROSSROADS

Turning right at junctions often causes some confusion when there is someone coming the other way who also wants to turn right. Do you cut across one another's bows, or go around one another? It really depends on the layout and width of the junction and how much more traffic is also waiting to turn. See Fig. 35.

Let us assume that you approach the crossroad cautiously, indicating "right" and positioning your bike correctly, close to the centre of the road. When you reach the junction you have to stop because of oncoming traffic, some of which wants to turn right, across your path. If there is room, and if more vehicles are likely to want to turn as well, it may be better that you turn in front of the other driver as in the lower half of the figure. This has some disadvantages. First, you had better be sure that he *is* going to turn. Second, it may not line you up with the crossroad. Third, you may not be able to see other cars coming from the opposite direction and they may well not be able to see you. The whole operation has to be conducted with some caution.

For all these reasons it may be more practical to adopt the other method (top half of Fig. 35) and go around the back of the other car — however, the disadvantage then is that if another car or two pulls up behind him and a few cars pull up behind you, you will all be stuck.

At the junction where you are going to have to choose one or

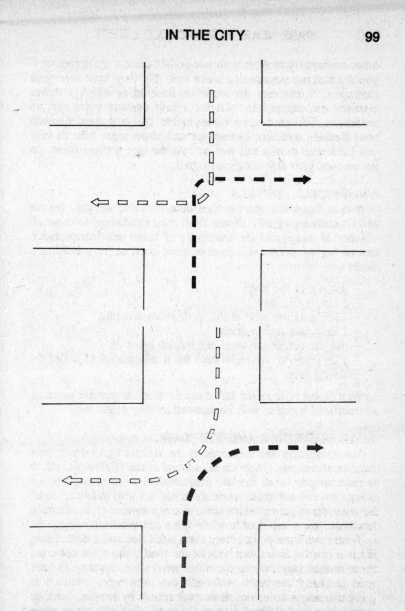

Fig. 35. It is necessary to allow room for other traffic when turning right at a busy junction. As the arrows show, you must choose either to go in front of one another or round the back of the oncoming vehicle, depending on the layout of the junction and the amount of traffic. Watch for oncoming traffic which is going straight on.

other method try to fit in with what other drivers are doing, or if you are making the running make sure that they *have seen* your intentions. Sometimes the angle or position at which a driver opposite has stopped to wait for a safe moment gives you an indication of the method he wishes to use. Use your eyes, maintain your flashing indicator throughout and allow extra time in case you are forced to stop half way out. As the next section warns, on no account give any unofficial signal.

UNOFFICIAL SIGNALS

It is at times like the one just described that naughty people make unofficial signals. People flash their headlamps to mean all manner of things and the ambiguity of intent and interpretation can be highly dangerous. Sample these reasons for a headlamp flash:

- get out of the way!
- I am giving way
- I am going to stop at this pedestrian crossing
- I have just seen a friend
- the car across the road has left its lights on
- I am going to turn right/wash the windscreen but I pulled the wrong lever ...

So it is not wise to put too much faith in the precise meaning of unofficial signals, well intentioned as they might be!

ROAD MARKINGS AND THE LAW

You must know the meanings of the various signs which have legal requirements. They are all set out in the *Highway Code*. It is quite easy to break the law unintentionally but saying you are sorry, you did not mean to do it, is not a viable defence. There are a couple of places which seem to catch motorcyclists out quite regularly; these are double white lines and zebra crossings.

Where there are double lines (or a solid line and a dotted line, if the solid line is on your side of the road), you must not cross these lines (except where there has been an emergency and the road is partly blocked). Although the lines were intended to prevent head-on collisions at normal speeds by keeping vehicles completely on their own side of the road, they still apply when traffic is crawling along. A motorcyclist filtering past could hardly cross the lines inadvertently, as they measure about half a metre across; if he does so it is an offence.

At zebra crossings there are zig-zag white lines painted along the edges of the road. You must not stop within these areas, other than to let people across the crossing, nor must you overtake the moving vehicle nearest to the crossing or the foremost stopped vehicle. You must give way to pedestrians on the crossing. Overtaking the lead vehicle is the part that can catch riders out — even if the definition of "overtaking" and "first vehicle" might boil down to technicalities, you could still get prosecuted. Parking in the zig-zag zone (even a little bike!) is also against the law.

Finally there is another variation on the double-white line theme, where cross-hatched markings are used to keep vehicles out of, e.g. a centre lane intended to shelter traffic waiting to turn right. If there is a solid line along the edge of the area, you must not ride over it. If the edge has a broken line, you may ride over it as long as you can see it will be safe.

9
Out-of-town Riding

Riding in the country takes away a lot of the pressures of traffic but in some ways this leads to a false idea of safety because when problems do arise they tend to be unexpected.

The open road and general lack of traffic means that speeds will tend to be higher and this can lead to problems in adjusting to the new speeds as well as having to change speed rapidly to cope with varying road conditions. In the city, the limiting speed is usually settled by traffic density or the speed limit prevailing; in the country within the overall limits of 60mph and 70mph it is often determined by the quality of the surface.

There are also long, empty straights punctuated by sudden corners, hidden junctions and humpback bridges. Someone who learned to ride out in the countryside would probably feel overwhelmed on his first ride through a large city. Yet someone who learned in the city would possibly be at greater risk in the country simply because he couldn't see all the problems that were facing him.

Surface hazards — even on main roads — tend to be seasonal. Mud is possibly the worst obstacle, deposited when the farmers are ploughing from autumn through to December and the biggest lumps always seem to be left on blind corners.

Leaves — very slippery — tend to gather through winter, and trees close to the road tend to shelter it, often leaving wet patches long after the rest of the road has dried out.

During those times when rain tends to bucket down keep a regular check on the bike, especially if you have to ride through a ford or flooded road. Water has peculiar effects on electrical equipment and on brakes. Make sure the brakes are working, and if they have been affected by the water, dry them out by riding slowly with the brakes gently applied. Similarly, check that all the electrical units are still working.

In the summer months the local authorities resurface the roads, spraying grit over the surface and leaving the traffic to roll it into place. Even after the surface has settled down, there may be broad triangles of loose gravel scooped up at road junctions or considerable quantities of stones deposited along the edges of roads. And, if there should be any hot summer days, the new tar will easily melt leaving a soft surface which isn't conducive to safe motorcycling.

Rain after a long dry spell always makes the road very slippery as it forms an efficient lubricant with the accumulated dust, rubber and oil. Bumps in the road and exaggerated road camber — often caused by heavy traffic damaging the road construction — add to these surface problems while humpback bridges have invariably got a tight turn or a T-junction on the far side.

Finally, the rate of growth of the hedgerows and verges in early summer is often enough completely to obscure road signs which might warn of bends, bridges or other forms of impending doom.

ANTICIPATION

Speeds on the open roads can be deceptively high; and even if it is possible to stop within the clearly seen distance ahead, it still helps to have some idea of what's coming next.

The lines of hedgerows, trees or telegraph lines often give an indication of where the road is going to go — although it's not a good idea to depend on it!

Because of the unpredictable nature of some of the roads, it is as well to leave a fairly healthy safety margin and to get all braking done before reaching corners, while the machine is still upright.

Fig. 36. Vanishing point, to judge speed and line into blind sections. Point X is where the road vanishes, over a crest in this case. If point X appears to be moving towards you, you are travelling too quickly and need to slow down until the point appears to hold a constant (or increasing) distance.

Fig. 37. Here the vanishing point is in a curve, obviously beginning as a right-hander. Positioning the bike to the left will increase vision into the corner; hold your line as long as point X is to the right, and adjust your speed until X appears to keep a constant, or increasing, distance from you.

There is a technique which is very useful for reading unfamiliar roads. This relies on the point at which the road vanishes from your view; over the brow of a hill, or in a corner where the line of one verge meets the other, as shown in Figs. 36 and 37. Call this vanishing point "X".

If point X appears to be moving towards you, then you are travelling too quickly and must slow down or brake immediately. If point X appears to be keeping a constant distance from you then you are travelling at a safe speed. In this case the scenery is unfolding at the same speed as you are travelling and you should be positioning yourself to get the best view or follow the smoothest/safest line through the curve, etc.

If the point X appears to be receding away from you then it is safe to start accelerating.

The only disadvantage of this technique is that it works so well that people trying it for the first time get fascinated by it and concentrate on it to the exclusion of the other things they should be doing!

Fig. 38 gives an idea of some more of the problems and some of the deductions which might be made from the scenery ahead.

The most deceptive roads are the fast, open A-class roads which are, fortunately, well-posted with warning signs and double lines. At fairly high speeds overtaking can take longer than you might anticipate and this may leave you travelling faster into the next bend than you'd bargained for, as well.

In addition to respecting double white lines, hold back, as the *Highway Code* urges you, wherever there are road junctions. In many cases the driver of a car approaching one of these junctions to join the main road will have a clear view to one side, while the view along the opposite stretch of road is obscured by hedges or trees.

Fig. 38. In the same way that traffic patterns can give you an idea of what is ahead, it is necessary to pick up as much information as possible from the open road. The line of the hedgerows and telegraph lines here suggests that there is a tight corner or a junction on the far side of the bridge which – in itself – causes the road to narrow. The gateway may mean that there is mud on the road and the shade provided by the trees often leaves damp patches after the rest of the road has dried out.

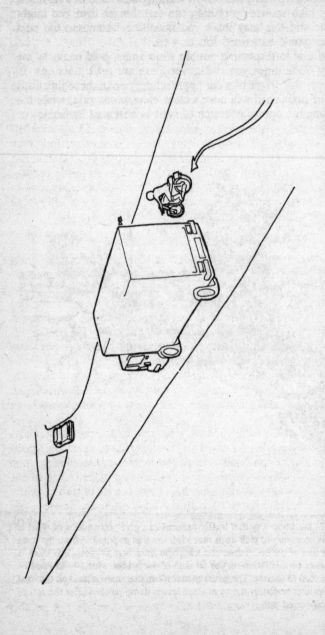

Fig. 39. Overtaking at open-road speeds may take longer than you think. There can be problems at junctions where the car driver can see to his right is clear and may swing leftwards onto the main road without stopping.

If he plans to turn left, and the clear view is to his right with no traffic, the danger is of his assuming that his intended lane to the left will be empty. His imagination does not stretch to allow for something from that direction being in the throes of being overtaken and he swings into the road to be confronted by two vehicles, side by side (see Fig. 39).

The difficulties in overtaking on country roads probably cause the most problems and the greatest dangers. With such limited opportunities drivers often get impatient and take chances; or a slower vehicle which cannot overtake the one ahead (or may fail to make proper use of his lower gears for acceleration) may selfishly travel closely behind, so that any other vehicle then has to overtake the pair of them. Before long there is a little convoy, and anyone who decides to try to get past it will probably have to cut in. The solution is, if you cannot overtake, leave a fairly large gap − or run the risk of someone making his own gap.

DUAL CARRIAGEWAYS

Motorways are also considered in this section as the only significant differences are that motorways are not interrupted by junctions, roundabouts or right turns and have certain restrictions on their use. Although learner riders and 50cc (or smaller) motorcycles are not allowed to use motorways some questions in the test may nevertheless require a thorough knowledge of motorway regulations to make sure you will be ready to use them once you pass.

Traffic joins and leaves motorways by slip roads which are always to the left of the main carriageway. These slip roads join the main road at a shallow angle, making, for a short distance, an extra lane.

This part of the road is meant to be used as an acceleration lane when joining the motorway. Use it to accelerate up to the speed of traffic in the left-hand lane of the motorway, regulating your speed and position so as to coincide with a gap in the traffic where you actually want to merge with it. If there is a lot of traffic, select a suitable gap to slot into. If traffic is light, either accelerate to get ahead of slower vehicles on the motorway or slow down to drop in behind them. Refer to Fig. 40.

Should you decide to slow down, check behind you first − there may be someone there who is expecting you to accelerate, or who may be looking back towards the motorway to find his own space in the traffic.

Similarly, if there is a vehicle in front of you, do not get too close to it, especially as you turn to look back. Even if the traffic on the motorway is heavy and all the vehicles are travelling closely together you should try not to stop on the slip road, except as a last resort – there is a very real risk of being rammed from behind. When traffic is unusually thick take the slip road slowly to begin with until you can identify a thinner patch and find a gap – then you should still have room to build up speed appropriately.

At complicated or dangerous motorway and dual carriageway intersections the traffic is often divided into streams by markings on the road and signs telling you not to change lane. Unless these are combined with directional route signs, the lanes will merge again on the other side of the junction, so just stay in your lane.

Where routes separate there will usually be at least two early warning signs showing you which lane goes where, so there should be plenty of advance notice. If you get the wrong route, do not be tempted to stop or to turn around through any gap in the central reservation; on a motorway that would be illegal. In any event, motorway or dual carriageway, you will not have to go far

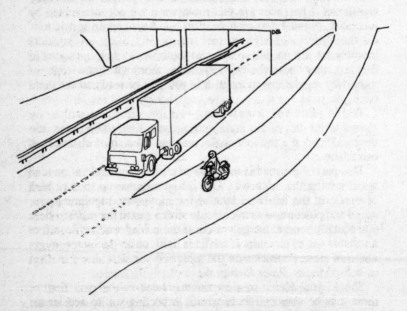

Fig. 40. Using a slip road to join a motorway or dual carriageway; the rider could either accelerate to get in front of the truck or slow down to drop in behind it.

before you can turn off. It might be a little further on a motorway but the problem could be avoided altogether if you check the route beforehand. If there is nowhere to carry a map or a route card on the machine, you can still make a note of any motorway junctions which you will encounter. All junctions are numbered and the numbers appear on maps and inside a small box on the motorway route signs themselves. All you need do is remember the junction number and the name of the town or number of the road you want. When that junction is due to appear make sure you slow down enough to read the direction signs clearly and get into the right lane.

If you're using a small motorcycle it is worth checking out any long motorway journeys beforehand against an up-to-date map. There are several stretches of motorway — particularly newly-built roads — which do not have any service areas for considerable distances. As the range of many motorcycles is limited, often to only 80 or 90 miles, it may be necessary to plan fuel stops quite carefully.

Up-to-date information on road conditions is usually available from the motoring organisations and from telephone services — look for the number in the front of the telephone directory.

When leaving motorways, and many dual carriageways, there is a similar slip-road arrangement which starts as an extra lane and then gently veers away from the main road. Often the junction itself will be a roundabout built either above or below the main road. If you're not sure whether it is the right exit, take it anyway. There will be more route signs at the roundabout; it will be far safer to stop there than on the motorway which, in any case, you are not allowed to do, and you can easily rejoin the original road again if need be.

The main thing when leaving a motorway is not to underestimate your speed. After long distances at steady high speeds, you can easily be deceived when you start to slow down. 40 or 50mph can seem ridiculously slow — until you have to stop. This is made more difficult when the slip road leads downhill to a roundabout or junction which goes underneath the motorway. In addition to the deceptiveness of the speed you will have the effect of the slope forcing you to brake just a little harder.

The same applies to the approaches to service areas. In all of these places other drivers have had to brake hard as well so the road is often quite well covered in rubber and oil deposits which can be fairly slippery, especially when wet.

Unlike motorways, dual carriageways have roundabouts,

crossroads and right turns directly off the carriageway. In this last case there is sometimes a slip lane, to the right of the right-hand lane but not always, particularly on older sections of road where the width of the central division has insufficient room for one. This means that there is every likelihood of traffic coming virtually to a standstill in the right-hand lane. Therefore, if a vehicle in the outside lane in front of you is indicating "right", it is essential to distinguish whether he merely means he is continuing to overtake slower traffic on the inside lane or whether he could intend to turn right. Leave a safe distance and keep to the left of the lane so that you will have plenty of time and room to avoid him if he does intend to turn right.

Similarly, if you have to take such a turning try to make your signals as clear as possible, slowing down well in advance so that you do not have to brake sharply and emphasising your intentions with an arm signal as well as the flashing indicators.

Other junctions, such as roundabouts or plain crossroads, often take people by surprise — partly because they are going faster than they realise — and it is not unusual to see people braking *more* abruptly than normal. As with motorway exits, the road surface often has slippery deposits or has been damaged by heavy use and is probably not the best place for heavy braking.

LANE DISCIPLINE

On all multi-lane roads you should ride in the furthest lane to the left; the next lane out to the right, and subsequent lanes, are for overtaking — or for changes of route, in which case they will be signposted. For normal use, the rule is to get past whatever it is you are overtaking and then return to the left-side lane.

Because of the (sometimes) enormous differences in speed between the slowest and the fastest vehicles on this type of road, it is essential to keep a continuous check in your mirrors. The scene behind you can alter very quickly and even if you are travelling at 70mph it is worth remembering that there are cars and bikes which are capable of travelling (illegally) at over 170mph.

When changing lane, or when joining a motorway, check the traffic behind and use the appropriate indicator. If you intend to move into the next of several lanes to your right, someone coming up in this lane will possibly also move one lane further over making room for you. However, do not assume that they will. Remember that unless you see them moving over in your mirror there could well be another car coming up overtaking them.

It will take some of the strain out of your journey if you can learn to judge relative speeds so that your overtaking on motorways can be done with the minimum of effort. Move into the right lane when there is a convenient gap some distance away from the vehicle you are going to pass. Try not to rush up behind it and have to pull out at the last minute − it could be going much more slowly than you think, or some faster traffic might appear behind you and prevent you from moving out, and you will have to stay in the same lane and brake. Then you will have to accelerate again when you finally get another chance to overtake.

MOTORWAY SPEEDS

Perhaps the most common problems associated with motorway or dual carriageway use are caused by the ease with which it is possible to hold high speeds. After a while this becomes deceptive both when you have to leave the motorway and when you have to stop or slow down unexpectedly. Very few people leave an adequate gap between themselves and the vehicle immediately in front; in bad weather or poor visibility the gaps are much too short − this and the deceptively high speeds can be the only explanation for each winter's series of motorway pile-ups.

Other problems are concerned with fatigue, especially as the motorway network allows people to cover really long distances with only the minimum of rest or exercise. Motorcyclists are particularly vulnerable in cold weather and may not recognise the danger signs, as the symptoms of both fatigue and hypothermia are apathy and a generally carefree outlook. It is better to make regular rest stops, walk about and have a hot meal or hot drink rather than to wait until you feel tired.

SURPRISE FAILURES

Any mechanical failure tends to come as a surprise − they always happen when you're least expecting them, when it is least convenient, and, on a motorway, you may be going fast. Whatever the problem − eespecially if it is something like a puncture − the important thing is to react decisively but not to over-react. Use the controls as smoothly as you can possibly can.

In most cases the answer is to stop − but to do it gently, not suddenly. If you have ever tried to brake hard on a flat tyre, you will know why it is fairly important to be gentle... Roll off the power and use the brakes gently, or not at all. If the problem is coming from the back wheel, ease in the clutch and if it is necessary to brake, use the front brake.

10
Riding in Poor Road Conditions

It is unfortunate that a book like this inevitably concentrates on the difficulties instead of the pleasures of riding motorcycles. However, while the enjoyment and the practicality are self-evident the risks are not always so immediately obvious. They present themselves suddenly, usually too late for the unprepared rider to get himself ready.

There are two factors which can make life difficult; bad surface conditions and poor visibility. Given our climate, they are often combined.

SURFACE

During the time you spend learning to handle your machine and with all the practice and experience you get, you should concentrate on learning the "feel" or feedback from the different types of surface, how it varies with different road materials and how it is affected by wet conditions.

These changes in the feel and response of the machine are due mainly to the effects of surfaces on the amount of inherent slip at the tyres, as explained in Chapter 6. The total amount of this slip will change on different surfaces and so will the proportion of slip between front and rear wheels. Designers allow for all this within limits but, tested too far, slip will inevitably develop into slide — on very bad surfaces there will be little or no transitional period to act as a warning; the tyres will slide in a trice unless the rider is extremely careful.

Sudden and unpredictable slides on treacherous surfaces can be avoided by making your riding as smooth as possible. This is particularly important where any changes are made, such as shifting gears and the instant when the brakes are first applied. Once you have the brakes on, it is much easier to feel the effect and to regulate the pressure delicately to give a fine degree of control.

It helps to change into a higher gear earlier and to pull the highest gear possible. This gives less torque magnification at the back wheel and a less fierce response to the throttle (see Chapter 3).

Where any extra stress is necessary, e.g. for braking, try to take it on the rear tyre more than the front. The reason is simply that if the rear wheel slides it is fairly easy to keep control of the bike. And when the back tyre breaks away, it does so relatively slowly. A front wheel slide is much more difficult to control and if the tyre breaks traction it will twist to one side very quickly.

On poor surfaces it therefore helps to make more use of the back brake in relation to the front than you would on good, dry surfaces. Also you must slow down much more before taking bends. This is because when the machine is steered through a corner, quite apart from the obvious need to be ridden more slowly than in good conditions, it improves traction if you can maintain gentle acceleration all the way through the corner. Without the extra reduction of speed *before* the bend this would be impossible.

As long as a slide does not happen too violently, it can be controlled. The tyre loses its grip when it is overloaded by too much cornering force (which acts sideways to the bike) or too much braking or acceleration force, which both act along the axis of the bike. Very often it is a combination of cornering and either braking or acceleration which overcomes the tyre's grip.

The cure is to reduce whichever force is causing the problem, by lifting the bike closer to the vertical, steering out of the corner, easing off the brakes or backing off the power. In each of these cases the correction has to be done gently for it to be effective. The tyre may well react to a sudden reduction as if it were a force in the opposite direction. This is particularly true if the bike starts to slide under power in a corner; slamming the throttle shut instead of gently easing it back will quite often make things worse.

The slide may not be caused by any direct action on the rider's part. It can happen simply as a result of the bike running across a slippery patch on the road. The tyres may grip again directly past the bad patch, or the slide, once started, may pick up its own momentum, with the bike continuing to slide even though the tyres are back on relatively grippy ground.

A typical example of this is a bike following a corner on a wet road, at a perfectly safe speed, and touching a cat's-eye which starts off a slide. Once the tyre has broken away there is a large drop in the friction available for grip between the rubber and the road surface. Sliding friction is always less than rolling or static friction and this factor does not help the rider to regain control once his bike has started to slide.

Apart from judging the likely grip of the road ahead by its appearance and through experience gained of such looking roads, the rider has no means of knowing how slippery it will be. The only safe way to add to our experience is to make allowances and always to assume the worst of a suspect surface, going slowly enough not to provoke a slide and allowing yourself plenty of time to see and avoid extra-slippery parts of it such as steel manhole covers, etc.

Developments in tyres, particularly for sports bikes, have given large increases in grip both in the dry and, more noticeably, in wet conditions. Tyre manufacturers often offer similar tyre sizes in different constructions and compounds, where the "touring" type will be harder-wearing and possibly more stable but will have less ultimate grip. These are sometimes called "hard" compounds.

"Sports" tyres, or "soft compound" tyres will have more grip, although at the expense of higher wear rates and probably a higher purchase price. These tyres might be less stable — a machine's steering will feel more nervous and twitchy and they might even cause slight weaving at high speed. As the tyres wear down, the centre of the tread wears more than the shoulders in road use and this changes the profile of the tyre. Because of this, the handling and stability may "go off" long before the tread pattern is worn down to the legal minimum. However, plenty of riders feel that the extra grip is worth the cost and the low mileage.

SNOW AND ICE

Riding carefully and smoothly will pay off in any conditions, particularly, as we have seen, when the surface is slippery. Two conditions are rare enough for us to get little practice at dealing with them, yet common enough to cause many crashes each year. These are ice and snow and although they are made of the same stuff they should be treated differently, if only because of their different appearances. Snow, unlike ice, is usually clearly visible and the first problem is, where to ride?

The hard-packed snow left by other vehicles is often firm and gives deceptive grip — you can accelerate and pick up a fair turn of speed — until you wish to stop or turn to one side, then the grip will disappear completely along with all pretence at steering and control. Fresh snow in modest amounts does give better grip as your tyres will sink through it to the firm ground underneath; the problem here is that you cannot see what is underneath and drifting snow can quite effectively disguise kerbstones and ditches. Also, after a short ride through fresh snow, the tyre treads

make allowances for the fact that you won't be able to notice surface changes quite so promptly.

It helps to have a powerful headlamp and keep it in good adjustment, remembering that as the front suspension compresses during braking, the light beam will be tipped down towards the road and will not give as much range as in the normal position.

You should use dipped beam at night whenever there is oncoming traffic and also when you come up behind someone else going the same way, otherwise your light beam will dazzle them via their mirrors. In town this will mean staying on dipped beam most of the time. In the country you must use main beam all the rest of the time. Switch up to main beam directly the reason for dipping has passed so that you lose no chances of seeing every detail of what lies ahead.

Powerful headlamps permit quite high cruising speeds, but dipped beam, on many machines, is rarely suitable for speeds above 50mph. This can lead to potentially dangerous situations which cannot be altered without a fundamental redesign because if the dipped beam is lifted then it will defeat its object and dazzle oncoming traffic. Consequently, it is possible to be travelling safely at high speed, and upon having to switch to dipped beam to find that you are then going 20mph faster than is safe. There is a tendency to ignore this and hope that there will be no obstacles − or to rely, for example, on an assumption that the vehicle which you have been following will not be able to proceed if there is any blockage on the road. There are flaws in this reasoning; to give just one − the thing blocking the road might well have fallen off the other vehicle.

3. Fog. This is one of the most frightening and disorienting experiences, especially if you run into a bank of fog without any warning. If there are no other vehicles around, there is not usually a problem as you can only go as fast as you can see and follow the kerb. Even so, it is possible to be travelling faster than you realise and even if you do not come across any unlit obstacle, it is not a bad idea to remind yourself that there could well be a parked truck or a skip only just in front of you. Never follow the central white line; there is an equal chance that someone coming the other way will have had the same idea.

It's surprising how many people only use sidelights in fog. The red tail-lights are usually visible (as are the high intensity rear fog lamps) but front sidelights are no more visible than the rest of the vehicle. In fog either a dipped headlamp or a fog lamp is essential and is legally required. If you're worried about someone crashing into the back of you, it doesn't hurt to flick the brakes on every few seconds not to slow you down, but just enough to light up the brake light.

And as long as you're sure there's no-one behind, it can be instructive to try a stopping experiment as soon as you see something in the gutter — a drain cover, say — imagine it is a somewhat larger obstacle and see if you can stop before you run into it.

By far the biggest problem associated with fog is other vehicles and the tendency to drive too fast and too close to them. Every year the newspapers have "motorway madness" headlines during the foggy season and motoring organisations and police patrols make scathing statements about the habits of the drivers involved. Yet it continues to be an annual feature in the statistics' books.

It's hard to believe there's anyone left in the country who hasn't heard of the perils and it's equally hard to believe so many people are just plain suicidal, so it seems likely that all the drivers involved believed they were behaving quite rationally.

The problem is probably that it is too tempting to follow a set of tail-lights and keep these red lights just within your range of vision. At this distance you may not be able to see the vehicle clearly and you are probably travelling too quickly for the conditions. BUT, you think you can still stop in the distance up to the tail-lights. Even if that vehicle stops dead, you believe you can still stop without hitting it. The reasoning so far, is rational. The other guy may be going too quickly, but that's his problem. You reckon you can take advantage of it at no risk to yourself.

The problem may be that you misjudge how quickly you can stop. Or there may be someone behind you who makes a misjudgement. Or, someone else may come along, following one set of tail-lights, catching the vehicle and then leap-frogging on to the next. After a while it begins to look easy and the speed creeps up; someone else decides they can follow the faster car and before long there's a small convoy, all of them not going too quickly but going much too quickly.

And it was all based, initially, on a logical judgement... All the drivers involved in those multiple crashes probably had, in the backs of their minds, a memory of how they'd been careful, how they were holding back and just staying with a set of tail-lights on the edge of their vision.

4. *Rain*. Wet roads cause bigger problems for motorcycles than for most other vehicles and this tends to produce bigger differentials in speed. Alternatively it can encourage riders to go

a little too fast and get that much closer to the limits. It also spoils vision, as raindrops settle on your visor, or smear when you try to wipe them off. A well polished visor reduces this problem and, at normal road speeds if you tip your head from side to side the airstream will blow most of the water off and save you the trouble of wiping it away.

Perhaps the worst part of riding in the wet is the spray kicked up by fast-moving traffic. On busy roads this can be really frightening — especially when you realise that everyone else must be suffering the same reduction in visibility, yet none of them appear to be reacting to it. Improvements in tyres' wet grip, in both trucks and passenger cars, are largely responsible. They pump the water off the road, giving safer road-holding but create another hazard in the spray produced. There are always a few who turn on their rear fog lights in these conditions (which is illegal unless visibility is less than 100 metres) and make matters worse — particularly at night — by dazzling the people behind them.

5. *Sunshine.* It is ironic that our major source of light should cause visibility problems, but it does, particularly when it is at a low angle on clear winter mornings and afternoons. The glare, either directly, or reflected from the road surface, can be dazzling, although the risk is quite obvious. The problems start when you turn from a shaded lane directly into the full light; or, when the light is behind you, you may forget that it is dazzling anyone approaching you. You can often judge ahead where the glare will be worst and slow down to prepare for dazzling when you reach it.

AQUAPLANING

Current motorcycle tyres cope with rain and wet roads extremely well and this is something for which we should obviously be grateful. However, this desirable performance does have one serious flaw. It makes us too confident. We tend to rely on the bike's properties rather than our own skills or judgement.

Tyres owe their grip primarily to the rubber compounds of which they are made. This presupposes that the rubber is in contact with the road and, on a wet day, that is where the tread comes into play, by splashing and draining water out of the way, so that contact remains consistent.

If at a constant speed the depth of water is slowly increased, there will come a point when the tyres cannot do this. New tyres can cope with a considerable depth but badly worn tyres cannot.

In the same way increasing speed makes matters worse on any particular degree of wet road because it means the tyre has to cope with a greater amount of water in a given time.

The effect, when a wedge of water builds up below the tyre and prevents contact with the ground, is called aquaplaning. In this condition the wheel is supported by a layer of water — which gives little in the way of steering or braking properties.

Given enough water in relation to speed or enough speed in relation to water, it can happen to any tyre so, as with most hazards, the best plan is to try to avoid it altogether. Do not ride through puddles; back off if the surface water gets deep enough to make splashes and spray. If puddles are large enough to be seen, they are large enough to be avoided (or at least, negotiated slowly) if only because you cannot tell how deep they are. Hitting a deep puddle at speed will slow the bike dramatically and may throw it out of control.

APPENDIX

USEFUL ADDRESSES
Commercial Scooter and Motorcycle Rider Training (CSM),
13 Eckersley Road, Chelmsford, Essex CM1 1SL.
Telephone 01245 359478

BMF Rider Training Scheme, PO Box 2,
Uckfield, East Sussex, TN22 3ND.
Telephone: 01825 712896

RoSPA, Cannon House, The Priory Queensway,
Birmingham, B4 6BS.
Telephone 0121 200 2461

Star Rider, 13 Eckersley Road, Chelmsford, Essex CM1 1SL.
Telephone 01245 495268

Department of Transport, 2 Marsham Street, London SW1P 3EB.

DVLA (Driver and Vehicle Licensing Agency), Swansea SA6 7JL.
Telephone Driver Enquiry Unit 01792 772151

Test application forms, etc – from large Post Offices, Traffic
Area Offices.

Local training schemes – see local dealers, Citizens' Advice
Bureau, local Road Safety Officer, Public Library, motorcycle
press.

Publications, regulations etc. – Traffic Area Office, local Road
Safety Officer, DVLA Swansea.

INDEX

LEARNING TO DRIVE IN PICTURES
by A Tom Topper

Packed with common sense and clear enough for a child of 12 to understand. It is lavishly illustrated and explains all the secrets that are at the heart of motoring safety and skill.

What to Watch out for when
BUYING A USED CAR
by Kenneth Salmon

Thousands of people buy second-hand cars each year. Sadly, many of them end up with vehicles which cost hundreds of pounds in repair bills. Make sure you're not one of them. Find out how to judge a car's merits, detect its faults and value it accurately. Whether you're buying from a private individual, from a car dealer or at auction, this book will save you money!

TEACH YOUR SON OR DAUGHTER
TO DRIVE
by David Hough

A book for learner and teacher to use together. It consists of ten lessons centred around in-depth analysis of the Highway Code. It sorts out what to teach, in what order and *how*. Amateur and professional instructors alike will welcome the way David Hough illustrates the correct teaching principles that most quickly develop a pupil's competence.

EMERGENCY CAR REPAIRS
by Martin Davies

Are you helpless when your car breaks down or won't start? If so, Martin Davies can help, He shows how you can do something *constructive* instead of having to wait helplessly for the breakdown service. From the humble puncture to the mystifying ignition fault, this is the perfect standby that can save you £££'s.

VERY ADVANCED DRIVING
by A Tom Topper

This book sets the advanced pace with its coverage of skidding, overtaking, emergencies, fast driving and continental driving. A Tom Topper writes with the authority of years of driving experience through snow, fog, ice, and rain, both at home and abroad.

RIGHT WAY
PUBLISHING POLICY

HOW WE SELECT TITLES
RIGHT WAY consider carefully every deserving manuscript. Where an author is an authority on his subject but an inexperienced writer, we provide first-class editorial help. The standards we set make sure that every **RIGHT WAY** book is practical, easy to understand, concise, informative and delightful to read. Our specialist artists are skilled at creating simple illustrations which augment the text wherever necessary.

CONSISTENT QUALITY
At every reprint our books are updated where appropriate, giving our authors the opportunity to include new information.

FAST DELIVERY
We sell **RIGHT WAY** books to the best bookshops throughout the world. It may be that your bookseller has run out of stock of a particular title. If so, he can order more from us at any time – we have a fine reputation for "same day" despatch, and we supply any order, however small (even a single copy), to any bookseller who has an account with us. We prefer you to buy from your bookseller, as this reminds him of the strong underlying public demand for **RIGHT WAY** books. Readers who live in remote places, or who are housebound, or whose local bookseller is unco-operative, can order direct from us by post.

FREE
If you would like an up-to-date list of all **RIGHT WAY** titles currently available, please send a stamped self-addressed envelope to

ELLIOT RIGHT WAY BOOKS,
KINGSWOOD, SURREY, KT20 6TD, U.K.